Paul's Apocalyptic Gospel

Paul's Apocalyptic Gospel

The Coming Triumph of God

J. CHRISTIAAN BEKER

FORTRESS PRESS   PHILADELPHIA

Library of Congress Cataloging in Publication Data

Beker, Johan Christiaan, 1924–
  Paul's apocalyptic gospel.

  Includes bibliographical references.
    1. Bible. N.T. Epistles of Paul—Theology.
  2. Eschatology—Biblical teaching. 3. Apocalyptic
  literature. 4. Church and the world. I. Title.
  BS2655.E7B44 1982   236   82–8670
  ISBN 0–8006–1649–9   AACR2

9600D82   Printed in the United States of America   1–1649

Contents

To
Terri Anne Kurosky-Beker
whose vocational work
stimulates
my theological
explorations

Preface

This book explores the challenge of Paul's apocalyptic gospel for the church. It owes its inspiration to three persons. First of all, after I had published my interpretation of Paul's apocalyptic in my book *Paul the Apostle: The Triumph of God in Life and Thought,* my friend Walter Wink urged me to address the question of the applicability of Paul's apocalyptic to the contemporary situation—in the manner in which Rudolf Bultmann had served post-World War II Germany. In the second place, conversations with my wife Terri and with my former colleague Cain H. Felder—both separately engaged in Christian social endeavors—compelled me to come to terms with the relevance of Paul's apocalyptic gospel for the church today, and its implications for ethical responsibility in our world.

These proddings then stimulated my personal and professional interest in the problem of apocalyptic. I discovered how Paul in his own career had wrestled with the proper delineations of his apocalyptic gospel and had sought to uncover its distortions by his audiences. And so I struggled with the relevance of Paul's apocalyptic gospel for our time, a time in which apocalyptic is *either* distorted into its Pauline opposite by apocalyptic sectarians *or* silenced and neutralized by the established church.

While researching the meaning of Paul's apocalyptic for our time, I realized that the two dominant motifs of my work on *Paul the Apostle* are applicable to this book as well. The first motif concerns the center of Paul's gospel and locates that "center" in Paul's Christian apocalyptic, which defines the content of Paul's gospel as the hope in the coming triumph of God.

The second motif specifies Paul's manner of interpreting the gospel. It claims that the uniqueness of Paul's interpretive method lies in his ability to allow the true content of the gospel to be relevant to the various and particular problems—"the contingent"—with which his churches were wrestling.

Paul's ability to allow an interaction to occur between the abiding "coherent center" of the gospel and "the contingency" of the particular situations that it addresses should be of great assistance to us today, faced as we are with a pluralistic diversity of Christian responses to the one truth-claim of the gospel of Jesus Christ. I hope that Paul's apocalyptic gospel may help us to discern the beckoning power of God's triumph in Christ. And I hope as well that in the light of that discernment we may live a life of allegiance to him who will defeat the powers of evil and death that seem to overpower our present world.

Finally, I would be remiss in not thanking the following persons: John A. Hollar of Fortress Press, who read the manuscript and many of whose suggestions have been incorporated into it, and similarly, Michael J. Roffina; Ms. Elizabeth G.W. Meirs for her patience in typing an often illegible script; and Ms. Teri Betros for her usual expertise in producing a final manuscript.

J. CHRISTIAAN BEKER
Princeton, New Jersey

1

The Lure
of Apocalyptic

For a long time now there has been a vigorous protest against
the apocalyptic mode of thought of the New Testament. Christians and non-Christians alike have felt alienated from a world
view that seems primitive and obsolete, that indulges in speculations about the end of the world, and that is preoccupied with a
literalistic understanding of fanciful images and bizarre visions.

Moreover, the predictions of apocalyptic prophets about the
end of the world have regularly turned out to be false because of
the stubborn continuation of history. How can preachers of the
gospel today seriously proclaim a future apocalyptic message
and hope to speak a word on target to their congregations? Who
would want to equate the message of the gospel with an obsolete
Jewish world view and contaminate it with a kind of hope that
has been refuted by the very process of Christian history? The
retention of an imminent hope in the apocalyptic manifestation
of the kingdom of God surely falls under Albert Schweitzer's
moving words about Jesus:

> . . . in the knowledge that He is the coming Son of Man, He lays
> hold of the wheel of the world to set it moving on that last rev-
> olution which is to bring all ordinary history to a close. It refuses
> to turn, and He throws Himself on it. Then it does turn; and
> crushes Him. Instead of bringing in the eschatological condi-
> tions, He has destroyed them. The wheel rolls onward, and the
> mangled body of the one immeasurably great Man, who was
> strong enough to think of Himself as the spiritual ruler of man-

kind and to bend history to His purpose, is hanging upon it still.[1]

Today, however, a new interest in the apocalyptic message of the New Testament is widespread. It is due to a variety of circumstances. There is not only a widespread uneasiness with the prevalent translation of New Testament eschatology in existentialist categories but also a growing awareness that a doctrine of unlimited progress for our culture turns out to be an illusion.

Questions addressed to the moral character of personal life are now transcended by more urgent global questions: will life continue at all for us on our planet? Moreover, technology and progress seem no longer to go hand in hand. To many of us, technology no longer represents progress, but instead—if not a regress—at least a threat to life itself.

And finally, the resurgence of the neo-apocalyptic movement not only registers how many people ask "apocalyptic" questions but also removes from our eyes the complacent attitude that constitutes our usual response to apocalyptic.

The church needs to speak with a clear voice on the subject of apocalyptic. It must cease from adopting a purely negative and defensive posture as if its only business is to criticize the irresponsible speculations of apocalyptic sectarians. Above all, it must cease from hiding itself in vague and foggy statements about the matter.

The lack of clarity on the subject of apocalyptic is clearly illustrated by a question-answer column in an authoritative Presbyterian magazine for the laity:

Q. Why are there so few sermons in our churches on the Second Coming? Is this part of our belief or not?

A. Not all Christians think alike on matters of theology, but it would be hard for someone to feel at home in our tradition, who did not understand God as the One who has come, who is present (Christ is risen) in our lives today, *and* who is yet to come in whatever form the future winds up taking. To literalize the Second Coming is to ruin both its beauty and its significance.

To ignore it is to avoid what may be the most important part of the Gospel we know about since the past and present, relatively speaking, are brief, while tomorrow borders on forever.[2]

In a subsequent issue of the magazine, a reader reacts to this statement:

> I compliment the Rev. _____ for his illusive non-answer to what I am sure was a serious question concerning the Second Coming of Jesus Christ. If I understood his answer, he said, in effect, "We don't all agree. But if you want to be comfortable in the UCC/UPC, you will need to agree that Jesus is coming again, but not really—for if you actually believe in the Second Coming you will ruin both its beauty and its significance. Yet you can't ignore it because it is in the future." Why not a simple answer? Why not admit that those who cannot receive the Bible literally must spiritualize the Second Coming because it is too large a segment of the New Testament to be ignored?[3]

I cite this extensive segment from the magazine because it illustrates not only the discomfort and vagueness of the responses of the clergy to apocalyptic questions but also the justified concern of the laity for clarity in these matters.

Our manner of treating the future apocalyptic of the New Testament in purely aesthetic terms or as an ornamental husk that adds poetic beauty rather than theological substance to our Christian convictions is both morally dishonest and intellectually shallow.

This book investigates the challenge of Paul's apocalyptic gospel for the church. It intends to clarify for the church what is at stake in adopting an apocalyptic stance. I am convinced that such a stance carries a rich promise for the relevance of the church's message for our time. I am also convinced that the definition of Paul's gospel as an apocalyptic gospel will invite considerable resistance. After all, the long struggle of the church with apocalyptic sectarians, its legitimate opposition to apocalyptic speculations, the neglect by apocalyptic sectarians of the christological foundation of the gospel, their ethical passivity and their restriction of salvation to an elite all give the term "apocalyptic" bad press.

In fact, the reader may well ask: Why use the term apocalyptic at all? Is it not more appropriate to call Paul's gospel an eschatological gospel? My reasons for using "apocalyptic" are twofold: first of all, the term "apocalyptic" guards against the multivalent and often chaotic use of the concept "eschatology" in modern times. Eschatology refers to "last things," but in modern use "last things" often refer not to things that come at the end of a series but to things that are final and ultimate. In other words, the use of the term apocalyptic clarifies the future-temporal character of Paul's gospel.

Second, apocalyptic denotes an end-time occurrence that is both cosmic-universal and definitive. Paul expects the future to be an apocalyptic closure-event in time and space embracing the whole of God's created order. Thus the term "apocalyptic" refers more clearly than the general term "eschatology" to the specificity and extent of the end-time occurrence.

Moreover, I hope to show that the usual connotations associated with apocalyptic do not apply to Paul's apocalyptic gospel. Paul is not commissioned to proclaim an arbitrary apocalyptic blast to the world, but to prepare the world for the redemptive coming of God, the one who has already come to us in his Son, Jesus Christ.

Chapter 2 discusses the modern apocalyptic movements of our time. It investigates not only the essential elements of their message but also the reasons for their popularity. It argues that, however distorted their message is from the perspective of the gospel, neo-apocalypticism senses the signs of the times and invites the church to a new reflection on the apocalyptic character of the gospel. The next chapter (chapter 3) delineates the apocalyptic character of Paul's gospel as he preached it to his churches.

Here I show that there are four major apocalyptic motifs that, however modified by the event of Christ, form the "coherent center" of Paul's gospel. These four motifs are *vindication, universalism, dualism,* and *imminence.* Whereas the motifs of God's vindication of his holy name and that of universalism point to the cosmic embrace of God's redemptive purpose, the motifs of dualism and imminence specify the present state of the Christian community as involved in suffering in the world and as motivated by an intense hope in God's final redemptive hour.

But how is Paul's apocalyptic gospel related to his apostolic career? Chapter 4 demonstrates that apocalyptic and ministry are inseparably related. Apocalyptic is not an abstract dogmatic proposition, but a living content that interacts with the particular needs of the churches to which Paul addresses his gospel.

I propose that Paul's apocalyptic not only provides the *content* of the gospel but also stipulates the *mode* of its preaching. This means that the mode of its preaching is dictated by a cruciform life in accordance with God's redemptive act in the death and resurrection of Christ.

The proposal that Paul's gospel is an apocalyptic gospel is defended against its detractors in chapter 5. Interpreters of Paul who opt for a different center of his thought argue that this center is located either in "realized eschatology," or in the cross of Christ, or in a form of salvation-history.

In rejecting these options, I must now face the crucial question: is Paul's apocalyptic gospel obsolete or relevant for the church? (chapter 7).

In order to make a case for the challenge of Paul's apocalyptic gospel, I discuss the four basic objections to Paul's apocalyptic: the obsolete character of the apocalyptic world view, the misleading "literal" language of apocalyptic, the argument that apocalyptic has a purely symbolic significance, and the refutation of future apocalyptic by the ongoing process of history.

The relation of theological to scientific method is especially important here because the social sciences tend to reject the theological claim of Paul's gospel, that is, its claim to be a word of God to confessing Christians. They do so either because they reject theological claims as subjective and arbitrary or because they absolutize their own psychological or sociological explanations.

If apocalyptic is inseparable from the center of Paul's gospel and if that gospel has a revelatory claim on Christians, then the promises of its challenge can now be presented. The final chapter (chapter 7) presents these challenges for the church as it finds itself in this world at this point in time, as follows: inasmuch as apocalyptic is an unalienable part of Paul's gospel, we cannot claim the integrity and power of Paul's gospel for our life today if we surrender his apocalyptic or neutralize its effect on his gospel. Apocalyptic, in sum, belongs to the substance of his gospel.

Paul's apocalyptic gospel is not to be defended on biblicistic grounds; rather it has a *catalytic* power for the church today, inspiring the church to a new reflection on at least six important theological issues:

One, Paul's apocalyptic makes an important contribution toward the worldwide ethical task of the church, once his apocalyptic is viewed not as an invitation to ethical passivity, but to active participation in God's redemptive will.

Two, it makes a contribution as well to the problem of evil and suffering in the world, inasmuch as Paul's apocalyptic gospel expects an ultimate resolution to the contradictions and sufferings of life in the coming triumph of God.

Three, Paul's apocalyptic anthropology with its cosmic and interpersonal dimensions opens up a vision of cosmic solidarity and of the interrelation of all of God's creatures. Paul's anthropology thus combats a narrow individualistic piety and a view that restricts salvation to the church.

Four, Paul's apocalyptic refuses to evaporate the coming triumph of God into a never-ending process of history or into a scheme that denies a finality to the future of the creation. Our life of anticipation is only then real when it is anchored in the coming actualization of God's triumph.

Five, notwithstanding the chronological embarrassment of the delay of the Second Coming (the parousia), Paul's apocalyptic gospel instills in us a new conviction and a new vision: the conviction that the triumph of God is in his hands alone and so transcends all our chronological speculations, and the vision that God's coming triumph will transform all our present striving and sighing (Rom. 8:17–39) into the everlasting joy of his glory.

And finally, the vision of God's coming triumph marks our time in history as an "apocalyptic" time in which the question of *either-or* displaces our inclination to distance ourselves from the crucial issues of our time. Over against our usual practice of accommodating ourselves to the values of our world, Paul's apocalyptic gospel demands the decision of our allegiance: either to the God of Jesus Christ or to the power structures of this world.

2

Modern Apocalyptic Movements

NEO-APOCALYPTICISM AND THE CULTURAL CLIMATE OF OUR TIME

This book aims to confront our times with the challenge of Paul's apocalyptic gospel. It will argue that Paul's apocalyptic message needs a new hearing in the church for the sake of the vitality of the church in our times. I call Paul's gospel an apocalyptic gospel because it looks forward to the final triumph of God in Christ over all those powers in the world that resist his redemptive purpose.

I am convinced that the authenticity of Paul's gospel is directly related to its relevance today and that whenever the integrity of Paul's gospel is suppressed or misunderstood, the power of the gospel is suffocated in our time. The center of Paul's gospel concentrates on the joyful news of the "gospel" that the death and resurrection of Christ have inaugurated the coming apocalyptic triumph of God. This triumph of God will resolve the ambiguities and contradictions of our historical life so that death "may be swallowed up by life" (2 Cor. 5:4). And the call of the gospel to its proclaimers consists in discerning the signs of the times in word and action so that people within the circumstances of their own lives may respond to the impetus of the Holy Spirit and move life in the direction of its glorious destiny in the kingdom of God.

In the course of Christian history the pulsating power of

Paul's gospel has frequently been misinterpreted and misunderstood. In various ways the apocalyptic hope of Paul's gospel was no longer considered to be an option for later audiences of the gospel throughout the Christian world. And because Paul's apocalyptic heritage, along with that of other early Christians, was not appropriated, apocalyptic had to find a home outside the established church in sectarian movements. One cannot help but be struck by the irony and sadness of this situation.

Although the established church had sound theological reasons for considering the apocalyptic sects to be a distortion of the core of the gospel, it had no ear for their legitimate impulse and so neglected to take them seriously. Conversely, the apocalyptic sects, driven out of the mainstream of the life of the church, often developed into pseudo-Christian movements, more intent on calculating the end-time, on withdrawal from the world, and on the salvation of an elite group than on the central tenets of the gospel of Christ. And so today when one contemplates the enormous popularity among Christians and curious outsiders alike of books like Hal Lindsey's *The Late Great Planet Earth* and *The 1980's: Countdown to Armageddon,* one is struck once again by the response of the established church. It is surely a misreading of both our cultural scene and the apocalyptic dimension of the gospel when the scholarship of the established church in its bewilderment over the enormous success of the neo-apocalyptic movement reacts by criticizing only its intellectual content and "primitive" hermeneutic. Rather it should acknowledge the astute ability of the neo-apocalyptic movement to read the signs of the times and to respond to the fears and hopes of ordinary people today. In other words, the success of neo-apocalypticism does not lie in its intellectual power but in its empathy with powerful elements of the cultural climate of our time. And before we utter our justifiable intellectual and spiritual objections we should ponder this question: to what extent have our mainline churches isolated themselves from the concrete stirrings of ordinary people in our culture by neglecting the proper apocalyptic dimensions of the gospel?

I will argue in this book that Paul's apocalyptic is diametrically opposed to neo-apocalypticism and unmasks it as a false Christian movement. Neo-apocalypticism also disguises itself in all biblical seriousness in order to appeal to some of the worst instincts of our fallen human condition. A proper understanding of Paul's gospel will show that a gospel based on God's redemptive act in the death and resurrection of Christ can tolerate neither a favoritism for the so-called elect nor a cosmic vengeance and doom for the nonelect. [1]

This indictment is not accompanied by complacency, however, but by a sense of sadness, just because a legitimate apocalyptic impulse—so blatantly neglected by the established church —is turned by neo-apocalypticism into a distortion of the truth of the gospel. It is important to understand that Paul's apocalyptic not only challenges the neo-apocalyptic movement but also the established church. That millions of people turn to neo-apocalypticism betrays not only the alienation of the established church from the fears and hopes of ordinary people but especially the church's inability to allow the apocalyptic dimensions of the gospel their full impact.

However, an analysis of the presuppositions that enable neo-apocalypticism to flower among us is perhaps as important as a critical analysis of the movement itself.

CULTURAL PRESUPPOSITIONS

What then are some of these presuppositions? Why is there, as it were, an apocalyptic climate in our time that preoccupies our thought—whether we turn to the book of Revelation and its prophecies or not?

It seems that the feeling of uncertainty, frustration, and dread in our time must be interpreted quite differently from people's earlier preoccupation with existentialism. Existentialism engaged itself with the meaning of human existence in the context of an absurd world. In its therapeutic form it led to "the triumph of the therapeutic," that is, to the acquisition of a personal survival technique and to a highly individualized definition of the meaning of existence.

At the present time a different mood pervades us. Whereas the existentialist posture questioned the *moral* value of life, we now have to face a more radical question. It is the question of life itself: will there be any life at all for us and our children?

In other words, apocalyptic and existentialist postures arise from different perspectives on life. Existentialists believe that the human question may be raised at the cost of the question of history and nature. They regard these latter questions as mute, peripheral, or uninteresting. The apocalyptic mood today senses that this perspective is no longer possible. Whether we want to accept it or not, human nature and the realm of nature are bonded together in an inescapable solidarity. This new sense of solidarity, however, is not a cause for joy but for deep anxiety because there is no guarantee that life will have a future, no hoped-for parousia, no Second Coming. We sense that humankind and nature will survive together or be destroyed together and that the likelihood will be the latter.

For this reason I consider our present cultural climate "apocalyptic" and not just pessimistic or despairing. We have the uncanny feeling not only that our present way of life may end but that the destruction of all life may be at hand. Although we are all familiar with the world of "private apocalypse," that is, the world of despair, disorder, and meaninglessness in our personal lives, we are now truly faced with a "cosmic apocalypse," with a world where our private apocalypse is conjoined with and determined by the destined doom of the world as such.

Apocalyptic sentiments are born in a time of "failure of nerve," a term used by Gilbert Murray to characterize the breakdown of rationality and order in the Hellenistic world.[2] They are caused by cultural crises and by such stupendous upheavals that our normal ways of perception and control are unable to adjudicate them. Whether we attribute apocalyptic stirrings to political, economic, or sociological causes, all these conditions can be summed up as follows: *apocalyptic is the product of a severe contradiction between legitimate expectations and reality.* The contradiction experienced between reality and expectations leads in turn to a type of crisis thinking that is no longer capable of mediating positions or rational adjustments but thinks instead in radical absolutes.

"Common sense" solutions no longer conform to the level of experienced crisis. Reality is now interpreted in terms of stark opposites—evil versus good, transient versus eternal, and so forth. When in a situation like this we still venture to hope, that hope is now directed toward a utopian, otherworldly apocalypse; and when we deem hope no longer appropriate, the future of our world is now viewed in completely destructive terms. And if we intermingle hope and hopelessness, we now hope for emergency exits from the world for an in-group so that "we" will be saved and "they" will be destroyed.

Our time is characterized by this "failure of nerve." It manifests itself in our disillusionment with technological progress, including the military-industrial complex, and with our inability to control the future.

In the face of nuclear destruction, environmental pollution, the limitation of natural resources, and ecological concerns, we are slowly but certainly forced to surrender the doctrine of progress that until now has constituted our version of the presence of the kingdom of God in history ("realized eschatology").

We suddenly realize that the apocalyptic conviction of early Christianity, which we so confidently had turned into a doctrine of infinite progress, rears its head again for us, albeit not in the form of promise but rather in the form of doom and destruction.

We are worried that we have lost control over our individual lives and cannot any longer determine our destiny, and we sense that evil and unpredictable forces turn the good we plan into the evil we desire to avoid.

I call this feeling "apocalyptic" because it engulfs both our view of the world at large and our private self. We seem inca-

pable of separating our private lives from their entanglements
with the economic, political, sociological, and biological spheres
of the world. And because that world offers no visible hope, we
feel paralyzed. The "end" of the world seems imminent to many
people and already to cast its shadows of doom in our midst.
The receptivity for neo-apocalypticism among us rests to a large
extent on some of these presuppositions. And we must be aware
of these apocalyptic stirrings in our culture in order to understand the profound impact of this movement.

Moreover, this receptivity is enhanced by the numerous predictions of doom promoted and commercialized by our dominant culture. Movies like *The Exorcist, The Omen,* and *Apocalypse Now,* advocates of survival and lifeboat ethics, and books
like William and Paul Paddock's *Famine—1957, America's Decision: Who Will Survive,* or Alvin Toffler's *The Eco-Spasm
Report* all proclaim a sense of doom and irrational evil.[3]

HAL LINDSEY'S "BIBLE PROPHECY"

Hal Lindsey's "Bible prophecy" intends to give to people who
are in disarray about a world gone out of control a rational hold
on the future of the world in the name of the gospel.

His version of apocalyptic provides not only a rational account of the terror that is befalling our world but also a prescrip-
tion for survival. And his "Bible prophecy" represents "absolute
truth" because it is derived from the one infallible source in an
utterly fallible and chaotic world: the inspired and infallible
word of God as transmitted in the predictive prophecies of the
Bible.

Neo-apocalypticism is based on a twofold assumption: a *predictability* of future events as prophesied by an infallible Scripture and a *divine determinism* that controls the precise events
leading to the end of history. Its chief attraction, however, lies
in its confident claim to correlate scriptural symbols and prophecies with contemporary events, with the result that Bible
prophecy dictates and approves a narcissistic preoccupation
with present world events as if they are the focal point of the

total historical process of humankind. The events of our time are neatly arranged pieces in a cosmic puzzle, and control over our threatening future is attained by a predictive knowledge—a kind of modern "gnosticism"—that is sure of itself because it knows the inexorable calendar of God's timetable as revealed in Scripture.

Lindsey's scheme is deceptively simple: he offers "the most thrilling, optimistic view of what the future could hold for any individual."[4] The Bible is the greatest prophecy book of all. "Bible prophecy can become a sure foundation upon which your faith can grow."[5]

In the Bible, prophets are tested by one criterion: did their prophecies come true? They passed the test fully as is evident in the fulfillment of the prophecies of Jeremiah, Ezekiel, and Isaiah. Moreover, the predictions of the Messiah, the time and place of his birth, his ministry, his rejection, betrayal, and suffering were all fulfilled in Jesus.

On the basis of all these fulfilled prophecies, we can be sure that the Bible's prophecies for the future are absolutely true as well. Lindsey's real interest lies in "the prophecies which are related to the specific pattern of world events which are precisely predicted as coming together shortly before the coming of the Messiah the second time—coming in power to rule the earth."[6]

Lindsey's pattern runs as follows: The reestablishment of Israel as a nation in 1948 and predicted by Ezek. 38:8 opens the drama of the end-time. It propels a realignment of the nations of the world into four spheres of political power (North, South, East, West); the repossession of ancient Jerusalem in 1967 by the Jews enables them to rebuild the temple on its old site. Pressure on Israel by a "northern power" (Magog = Russia) and by the King of the South (Ezek. 38:2; Dan. 11:40; = Arab alliance) leads to increasing wars, even thermonuclear exchanges centered on the crucial "land bridge" of the world, the plain of Megiddo.[7] According to Daniel 7 and Revelation 13, Antichrist will become increasingly powerful: he sets up an absolute dictator in a United Europe (the revived Roman Empire = the Common Market) and prepares for the final onslaught between the West (United Europe) and the East (the hordes from China) after the North and South (Russia and the Arab alliance) have been defeated with supernatural help before the gates of Jerusalem. Around this time "the rapture" will occur, "the ultimate trip" for all believers. It will take place before the seven-year tribulation that will climax in Armageddon—the ultimate destruction of the world by nuclear destruction. At this point Jesus Christ (the Messiah) will return from heaven accompanied by the true believers to bring about his millennial kingdom, to be followed by the last judgment and the eternal kingdom of God.

How shall we evaluate this apocalyptic interpretation? In the first place, Hal Lindsey's description of the coming fate of "The Late Great Planet Earth" is deterministic in the extreme. Nothing can change the spinning of the wheel of apocalyptic destiny. His characterization of Christian hope provides no sense of participation, no sense of responsibility in the world events that march inexorably toward utter destruction. Christians are not called to engage in working for peace, understanding, and reconciliation among the nations. All this is simply an exercise in futility. The cosmic favoritism for the elite suffocates the sense of human solidarity so dominant in the gospel. Christians are not redemptive agents in the world, but "Gnostics" who must attend to God's timetable. They know what is going to happen and they are able to sit back calmly and watch the apocalyptic events unfold. And those events have a great urgency because the timetable of history will come to an end—very shortly.*

Second, Lindsey's apocalyptic is totally devoid of a christo-

---

*Daniel L. Migliore remarks: "Since Jesus in Matt. 24:34 said that 'this generation' (i.e., the generation alive when the nation of Israel was re-established in 1948) would not pass away until all would be fulfilled, and since a generation in biblical times is about 40 years, Lindsey is in effect predicting that the world will be destroyed by thermonuclear war no later than 1988. However, since there is a seven-year period of tribulation *before* the end, this is presumably to commence no later than 1981. These are my figures rather than Lindsey's, but they are based on what he says, and we have to conclude that Lindsey expected his readers to make these simple arithmetic calculations." "Theology of Hope," unpublished lecture, Princeton Theological Seminary (Fall 1979).

logical focus. The story of Jesus Messiah (= the Christ) becomes simply a part of the demonstration of the accuracy of biblical prophecy. The result is that the significance of the death and resurrection of Jesus Messiah in the determination of the future for which Christians hope is unclear. Therefore, speculation about the final events of history and the return of Jesus Messiah runs rampant.

Third, Hal Lindsey builds his case on what someone has called "apocalyptic inoculation": [8] the biblical materials he cites are totally divorced from their proper historical contexts. Moreover, his method of biblical interpretation is literalistic in the extreme. The apocalyptic sections of Scripture provide the insider with a detailed referential code of present world events.

Furthermore, the real Christian hope lies in "the rapture," which must be characterized as a form of "apocalyptic terrorism." "He has frightened the hell out of us. Two hundred million Chinese soldiers backed by nuclear weapons destroy one-third of the earth's population." [9]

However, there is hope! Believe in Jesus Messiah as your Savior and you will be raptured and escape all these horrors. "This is self-centered hope in the extreme. There is no sense of solidarity with a creation and humankind groaning for emancipation from its suffering." [10]

Finally and most important of all, there is *no theology of the cross* in this apocalyptic. For when the world suffers its worst tribulation, the church will be in heaven. Whereas the center of Lindsey's hope is a future event called "the rapture," the center of New Testament hope is the resurrection of the crucified Jesus. "If any man would come after me, let him deny himself and take up his cross and follow me" (Mark 8:34). Indeed, as Paul says, "The love of Christ controls us, because we are convinced that one has died for all; therefore all have died. And he died for all, that those who live might live no longer for themselves but for him who for their sake died and was raised" (2 Cor. 5:14–15). The hope of the Christian, then, has been cleansed from all wishful thinking by the cross of Christ.

THE CHALLENGE OF
PAUL'S APOCALYPTIC GOSPEL

Criticism of this sort certainly must be leveled against the Christian pretensions of neo-apocalypticism. And it is all the more necessary when one observes the popular, folksy, "catchy" style and spirit of Lindsey's books. Part of this popular appeal undoubtedly lies in the pernicious manner in which Lindsey appeals to the deep-seated fears of his readers and cashes in on the apocalyptic stirrings in our culture. And so the charge of "apocalyptic terrorism" is quite to the point.[11] Moreover, all this predicted horror is described in an almost joyful tone, as if the destruction of our precious God-created world is nothing but a computer printout in which the Christian elite have no participation whatsoever because of its predicted ultimate trip—"the rapture."

Legitimate criticism, however, should not make us complacent or blind to the sad fact that respectable theologies of the established church have continuously dismissed apocalyptic from their own theological agenda and are thus indirectly responsible for the distortions of neo-apocalypticism among us. For the apocalyptic silence of the established church certainly left the vacuum that this movement now fills. Therefore, however distorted Lindsey's apocalyptic scheme is from a Christian perspective, it should not only stir us to indignation but also motivate us to a new reflection. A distorted apocalyptic is not to be met by the traditional nonapocalyptic response but by the challenge of a Christian apocalyptic that mainline Christianity has repressed far too long. Paul's apocalyptic gospel presents such a challenge. It not only corresponds to the truth of the gospel but also promises to give it new power among us.

3

The Apocalyptic Character
of Paul's Gospel

I will now argue that Paul's apocalyptic gospel not only challenged his own time but also challenges ours. I select Paul's gospel for both historical and theological reasons. Paul is the earliest literary figure of the New Testament and represents an impressive example of the pristine power of the gospel in apostolic times. His interpretation of the gospel is dominated by two features that the church today needs to hear anew.

In the first place, the abiding center of Paul's gospel is the conviction that the death and resurrection of Christ have opened up a new future for the world. This future climaxes in the reign of God as that event that will bring the created order to its glorious destiny according to God's promises.

In the second place, Paul's proclamation of the gospel conforms to its apocalyptic shape. He was able to preach the gospel of God's coming glory in such a way that it inserted itself into the concrete and various particularities of people's lives. And so he enabled people to discern the glorious rays of the coming kingdom and to work redemptively in the world in order to prepare it for its glorious destiny.

In order to understand the ancient and modern challenge of Paul's apocalyptic gospel, we must first of all sketch its main components. For unless we have a clear picture of the contours of that gospel in Paul's own time, we will not be able to achieve its transfer into our time.

THE BASIC STRUCTURE
OF PAUL'S APOCALYPTIC GOSPEL

Paul's apocalyptic gospel is constituted by certain apocalyptic components that he derives from his Jewish apocalyptic world and that he radically modifies because of his encounter with Christ and the Christian tradition that he inherits.

Jewish apocalyptic is a literary phenomenon that arose in Judaism in the second century B.C. The period within which Jewish apocalyptic flourished was a period of martyrdom for the Jewish people. The central question that occupies the apocalypticist is how to overcome the discrepancy between what is and what should be. Why is faithfulness to the God of the Law rewarded by persecution and suffering? Questions like this come to expression in a literature that uses a variety of literary forms: dreams, visions, surveys of world events, descriptions of coming woes and of a final redemption.

Although Paul severely reduces the imagery of apocalyptic descriptions, he centers his thought on four basic components of Jewish apocalyptic: the motifs of *vindication, universalism, dualism,* and *imminence.*

Vindication

Paul's proclamation of Jesus Christ (= the Messiah) is centered in a specific view of God and in a salvation-historical scheme. What does that mean? It expresses the conviction that, in the death and resurrection of Jesus Christ, the Covenant-God of Israel has confirmed and renewed his promises of salvation to Israel and to the nations, as first recorded in the Hebrew Bible. These promises pertain to the expectation of the public manifestation of the reign of God, the visible presence of God among his people, the defeat of all his enemies and the vindication of Israel in the gospel. In other words, the death and resurrection of Jesus Christ manifests the inauguration of the righteousness of God. As Ernst Käsemann has shown, the righteousness of

God signifies both God's gift in Christ to his people and the claim of the sovereign Creator to his world. [1] That is, the issue of God's vindication of his honor and name are at stake as the hallmark of his promise to Israel—powerfully expressed in the Psalms and Ezekiel. Will God prevail, will he uphold the claims he makes?

> For thy name's sake, O Lord, preserve my life! In thy righteousness bring me out of trouble! And in thy steadfast love cut off my enemies (Ps. 143:11, 12ᵃ).

> Therefore thus says the Lord GOD: Now I will restore the fortunes of Jacob, and have mercy upon the whole house of Israel; and I will be jealous for my holy name (Ezek. 39:25; cf. 39:7, 21).

> It is not for your sake, O house of Israel, that I am about to act, but for the sake of my holy name, which you have profaned among the nations to which you came. And I will vindicate the holiness of my great name . . . ; and the nations will know that I am the LORD, says the Lord GOD, when through you I vindicate my holiness before their eyes (Ezek. 36:22–23).

These statements occur in a specific setting because the history of Israel was marked by serious questions about God's power and presence. Especially since the exile (587–538 B.C.) faithfulness to the God of Israel was met by persecution, death, and suffering; indeed, empirical circumstances showed that God's enemies were in charge of the world.

It is in the context of Israel's yearning for God's vindication over the created world that Jesus Christ is proclaimed as the manifestation and confirmation of God's faithfulness to his redemptive plan—the Messiah of God. And so Paul proclaims in 2 Corinthians:

> For all the promises of God find their Yes in him. That is why we utter the Amen through him, to the glory of God (2 Cor. 1:20).

Christ is here presented as the manifestation of God's *Amen* (the Hebrew equivalent of the Greek *Yes*), that is, as the symbol of God's faithfulness to his promises.

This christological proclamation cannot be understood simply in terms of a promise-fulfillment scheme, as if Christ—the "Yes" of God—is the climax of God's self-vindication. This would represent a spiritualization of the eschatological promise, as if God's self-vindication and faithfulness to Israel occur in a sphere which leaves the structures of the history of the world untouched. In order to resist such a misunderstanding, Paul insists that the present gift of the Spirit is not the full payment of the promises of God, but their guarantee (2 Cor. 1:22). The emphasis on God's self-vindication and faithfulness to his promises, then, must be understood within the framework of Paul's description of God. It is important to stress this because Paul is seemingly so preoccupied with *Christo*-logy and so little interested in an explicit *theo*-logy that it is easy to misconstrue his theology as Christology and to forget the theocentric, that is, the God-centered texture of his thought. It is *God* who in Christ triumphs.

An important insight into Paul's description of God is afforded us in Rom. 4:17. Abraham is said to stand "in the presence of the God in whom he believed, who gives life to the dead and calls into existence the things that do not exist." God is here characterized as the Creator and eschatological Redeemer—the one whose sovereignty at the beginning of creation will be matched by the vindication of that sovereignty at the end of creation. This typically Jewish formulation is not a philosophical description of the nature of deity but a confessional exclamation, as is evident, for instance, in 2 Cor. 1:9, where Paul contrasts self-reliance in the face of his own possible death with reliance on "God who raises the dead."

The faithfulness of God has been inaugurated in Jesus Christ, and therefore God's public self-vindication as the climax of his faithfulness to himself and his world is imminent. The "faithful" (*pistos*) clauses in Paul's letters confirm this:

He who calls you is faithful, and he will do it (1 Thess. 5:24).

God is faithful, by whom you were called into the fellowship of his Son, Jesus Christ our Lord (1 Cor. 1:9; cf. 2 Cor. 1:18).

And so the "faithlessness" of Israel cannot "nullify the faithfulness of God" (Rom. 3:3)—that is, God's self-vindication: "Let God be true though every man be false" (Rom. 3:4a). God, the "Father of our Lord Jesus Christ" (Rom. 15:6; 2 Cor. 1:3), is the one who spans the time from the creation to the end-time and governs the created world with absolute sovereignty. "For from him and through him and to him are àll things. To him be glory for ever" (Rom. 11:36).

Paul would have agreed with the author of Revelation, when he lets God speak: " 'I am the Alpha and the Omega,' says the Lord God, who is and who was and who is to come, the Almighty" (Rev. 1:8). And he would have sung with the twenty-four elders of the Apocalypse:

Worthy art thou, our Lord and God, to receive glory and honor and power, for thou didst create all things, and by thy will they existed and were created (Rev. 4:11).

The faith of the Christian community is grounded in the overarching redemptive plan of God, who alone determines its execution and who alone did determine the fullness of time, in which his Son appeared to inaugurate the liberation of the created order. And so the Christian church utters the Amen in response to the *Yes* (= Amen) of God's action in Christ (2 Cor. 1:20). Faith (*pistis*) can be characterized simply as the "Yes" to God's faithfulness (*pistis*); indeed, the response to God's trustworthiness constitutes the trust and confidence of the church:

And I am sure that he who began a good work in you will bring it to completion at the day of Jesus Christ (Phil. 1:6).

In fact, faith, according to Paul's letters, regularly spills over into hope (Rom. 4:18, 5:3–5, 8:25; Gal. 5:5; 1 Thess. 1:3) and is frequently associated with endurance, patience, and waiting. This interrelationship demonstrates the apocalyptic perspective

of Paul's gospel. Faith and hope are not merely synonymous in
the sense that both terms participate in the attitude of trust as
the religious stance of the believer. Rather they are interrelated
because both are directed to the object of the hope—which is
God's vindication at the end-time. "Faith in Christ" then is an
abbreviation for "faith in the God who in Christ's death and
resurrection has redeemed us from the bondage of sin, and has
transferred us to the dominion of his righteousness" (Rom.
3:21-26). Paul characterizes Jesus Christ as the pledge of God's
imminent self-vindication, and thus faith in Christ describes
that reality of hope that is able to bear the tension between our
confession of God's righteousness and the empirical reality of
our world. [2]

In short, Paul's gospel is anchored in a theocentric, that is,
God-centered, view of the universe. And the manner in which he
interprets this theocentric view marks him as an apocalyptic
theologian. Consequently, Paul's interpretation of the gospel is
an interpretation in the mode of hope because he believes in the
God of Israel whose self-vindication and faithfulness to his
promises have been inaugurated in the death and resurrection of
Jesus Christ and will shortly be fully actualized in his creation.

Universalism

The apocalyptic motif of universalism—or the cosmic extension
of God's majesty and glory—involves Paul in a profound modi-
fication of its place and character in Jewish apocalyptic. The expectation of God's universal reign in Jewish apocalyptic is
anchored in the self-awareness of Israel as the people of the elec-
tion, the covenant, and the Law (the Torah). God's vindication-
and-faithfulness is primarily directed to the vindication of those
in Israel who are faithful to the Law of God. Thus Israel's hope
directs itself to the reversal of its present distress among the nations; and the reverse side of the hope is Israel's vindication before and over against the powers of the nations that oppress her.
And even when Israel views the messianic era in terms of a pil-

grimage of the Gentile nations to Jerusalem (Isa. 2:2-3; Mic. 4:1-2), Israel's thinking remains introverted rather than extroverted. Although Israel can contemplate a new covenant with her God in the messianic era, the notion of a new Torah or its abrogation is abhorrent to her. This same correlation of apocalyptic vindication and nationhood marks Israel as a basically nonmissionary religion and accounts to a large extent for the vengeance motif in its portrayal of the end-time. It will be a time of a radical reversal of all existing values: the powers of this present age with all their present might and glory will be destroyed, and the powerlessness and tribulation of Israel will be changed into its opposite. New values will replace the established ones.

For Paul, God's intervention in Christ profoundly modifies this apocalyptic motif. The division in humankind is constituted not by those faithful to the Torah and those who are wicked and "Gentile sinners" (Gal. 2:15) but rather by the death of Jesus Christ as the focal point of God's universal wrath and judgment. The death of the Christ signifies the apocalyptic judgment on all humankind, whereas the resurrection signifies the free gift of new life in Christ for all. This estimate of the death of Christ enabled Paul to radicalize not only the effect of God's wrath but also the sway of the powers of sin and death. There can be no favorite-nation clause or claim to privilege before the apocalyptic judgment of God in the cross of the Christ. Those "who belong to Christ" (1 Cor. 3:23; 15:23) have passed through the abyss of God's judgment; they have been baptized into Christ's death and have been buried with him (Rom. 6:3-4). Although this radicalization of the human condition in the cross of God's Messiah logically seems to lead to a conception of universal salvation, Paul refrains from any unequivocal assertion of this point. The time between the cross and the end-time is a time for commitment, decision, mission, and endurance. Those who are disobedient to the gospel will be judged and destroyed in the last judgment because they behave as if the powers defeated by Jesus

Christ still rule the world. Thus the thrust toward a notion of universal salvation is balanced by an emphasis on responsibility and obedience for those who have heard the gospel.

The first aspect of Paul's universalistic motif, then, is the rejection of any elitism, because the cross as God's universal indictment of humankind eliminates such a notion. Moreover, three other aspects of this motif characterize Paul's gospel. Paul interprets the cosmic-universal rule of God in the context of (1) a cosmic anthropology and of (2) a cosmic righteousness, and hence of (3) a concrete ethic.

(1) Ernst Käsemann has pointed out that for Paul "anthropology is cosmology *in concreto.*"[3] He means by this rather dense phrase that for Paul the human being is involved in the worldwide conflict between the kingdom of God and the kingdom of this world. In other words, for Paul there is no dualism between the human soul and the external world. He places the human being in the context of the world and its power structures. And because the person is viewed from a cosmic perspective, a profound solidarity and interdependence exists among the people in the world, a solidarity which even reaches into the realm of nature. In other words, the various parts of the created world are mutually related to each other and form a united whole. This means that, until all of God's creation comes to its destiny of glory, neither God himself is vindicated nor the human being completely or fully "saved."

Because the cross of Christ signifies a universal judgment, all people must die "in Adam" and all people are "flesh" (Rom. 5:12–19; 7:5; Gal. 5:16–17). And although Christians are redeemed from the power of the flesh, they must still live in the flesh as part of their solidarity with a world that is still subject to the powers of the flesh, sin, and death (Rom. 8:4; 2 Cor. 10:3; Rom. 8:18–25).

What is truly amazing in Paul is that he is able to correlate a profound analysis of an individual's existence before God (Rom. 7:7–25) with a cosmic-universal view of humanity in all its social and biological dimensions (Rom. 8:18–30). In other words, Paul's cosmic anthropology enables him to overcome a bifurcation between the personal and social aspects of the gospel.

This bifurcation all too often plagues our Christian life when, for instance, personal spirituality is set over against the "social gospel."

(2 and 3) Paul's cosmic anthropology, then, has profound implications for Christian ethics. This becomes clear in Paul's development of an apocalyptic ethic based on the universal scope of God's righteousness. God's *gift* of righteousness is inseparable from God's *claim* on his created world, and that claim will be actualized when all parts of God's creation participate in his glory, that is, when the era of *shalom* or cosmic peace and the reconciliation of the world will have actualized God's justice on earth. In other words, for Paul God's gift of righteousness in Jesus Christ is not to be divorced from his claim on us for righteous action.

This has important consequences for the ethical stance of the Christian in the world. Negatively, it means that there will be no place in God's kingdom for the isolated self or for the selfish. The ethnocentricity of Judaism with its dividing wall of the Torah is broken down, just as all forms of Christian elitism or of Christian self-fulfillment *over against* the world of the other creatures of God are rejected. The universal future scope of God's coming reign, then, accounts for a radical conception of the church *for* the world. Christians are obliged to become partners in God's cosmic redemptive plan: their ethic cannot be an ethic of excess, in the manner of a philanthropic condescension of the "haves" toward the "have-nots." For, according to Paul's teaching in Rom. 8:17–39, as long as the creation groans, Christians groan as well. And the groaning is motivated not so much by sympathy on the part of those who supposedly "have got it made" as by a conviction of solidarity. Christians must know that as long as any section of God's creation suffers, they cannot and should not as yet participate in the eschatological glory of God. For this reason the issues of the last judgment and of the final resurrection are not peripheral matters to Paul. We are all held accountable to God at the last judgment for our stewardship of God's creation, just because Jesus Christ has enabled us by his grace to be responsible. To say it in eschatological terms: we pervert Paul's God-centered vision when we adhere to a false Christ-centered perspective. In that case, we fuse *Christo*-logy with *theo*-logy and eclipse the doctrine of God from our thought.

The consequence of such an eclipse is that we suppose that all things already *have been* accomplished in Christ so that the knowledge of *our* salvation is all that matters—as if our only concern with the world should be a view of the world as the stage and platform for our own striving for sanctification.

The universal embrace of God's reign then denotes the depth and breadth of God's self-vindication because God wills his self-vindication only in and through the vindication of all his creatures:

> The glory of the Lord shall be revealed, and all flesh shall see it together (Isa. 40:5).

> For as the earth brings forth its shoots, and as a garden causes what is sown in it to spring up, so the Lord God will cause righteousness and praise to spring forth before all the nations (Isa. 61:11).

―――――――――――

Thus far we have investigated the dual apocalyptic motifs of *vindication* and *universalism*. They were shown to be interrelated, inasmuch as the universal motif defines the depth and cosmic embrace of God's self-vindication as the vindication of his created world.

Paul employs two other apocalyptic motifs in his presentation of the gospel. The motifs of *dualism* and *imminence* specify the present state of the Christian community as involved in the oppressive structures of the world and as motivated by an intense hope in God's final redemptive hour.

Dualism

What then is the precise meaning of the motif of dualism? It specifies not only the obstacles—the powers of evil—to the universal vindication of God's plan of salvation but also describes its anticipated character in the present—the power of the Spirit in our midst—in a provisional way.

In Jewish apocalyptic the motif of dualism expresses the antithesis between this world and the world to come, and the hostility of the forces of evil in our world to representatives of the coming age of God's kingdom. This antithesis is born out of a deep existential concern and expresses in many ways a theology of martyrdom. The apocalypticist is profoundly aware of the discrepancy between what is and what should be and of the tragic conflict between faithfulness to the Torah and its apparent futility. He or she lives a hope, therefore, that seems contradicted by the stubborn realities of this world, but that is nurtured by faith in the faithfulness of God and in God's ultimate self-vindication. The dualism between "this age" and "the age to come" must be understood in connection with the cosmic anthropology of apocalyptic (see p. 36, above). The forces of evil that dominate the present world are both macrocosmic and microcosmic powers: the angelic forces under Satan rule not only the world of history and nature but also the inner being of persons. This has come about because the fall of Adam and of humanity as well has caused the fall of nature and history. And so Satan and the cosmic powers of darkness occupy both the soul of the world and the soul of humankind. However, in the coming age of God's kingdom, not only humankind but also the world of nature will be radically transformed and so participate in God's glory, that is, in God's vindication of his creation. The world will be transformed into the glory of paradise and humans will be clothed with a new, incorruptible body of glory.

Paul's Christian apocalyptic modifies the Jewish apocalyptic motif of dualism by both tempering it and intensifying it.

(1) He *tempers* it because the history of Israel is for him not simply the old age of darkness. Israel's past contains the footprints of the promises of God, and these promises are taken up into the new age rather than cast aside. Thus Paul *softens* the dualism between the present age and the age to come by interpreting Israel's history in a typological way. The era of "the old covenant" has its own (temporary) "splendor" (2 Cor. 3:7-11); the exodus story has eschatological meaning for believers (1 Cor. 10:1-13); the privileges of Israel are real and abiding (Rom. 9-11); and although Christ is the end of the Law (Rom. 10:4), the Law is "holy and righteous and good" (Rom. 7:12) and plays a necessary part in salvation-history.

(2) Moreover, the death and resurrection of Christ mark the incursion of the future new age into the present old age. Thus the Christ-event has strongly *modified* the dualistic structure of Jewish apocalyptic thought. Already the powers of the new age are at work in the church and already believers can resist the "deeds of the body" (Rom. 8:13) because of the presence of the Spirit—the sign of the new age—in their midst. Indeed, the Spirit enables "a new creation" to occur in the midst of the old creation (2 Cor. 5:17), and this manifests itself in "signs, wonders and mighty works" (2 Cor. 12:12; cf. Rom. 15:17-19) and in glossolalia, prophecy, and healings (1 Cor. 12:4-11).

The dualism between the old and new age, then, is *tempered* in the first place by Paul's stress on continuity in the midst of discontinuity with respect to God's continuing faithfulness to Israel. In the second place, the incursion of the new age occurs in the midst of the old because of the new life brought about by Christ's death and resurrection.

(3) From a different perspective, however, the dualism is *intensified* as well: just because the forces of the future are already at work in the world, the confrontation in the present world be-

tween the powers of death and the powers of life aggravates *the crisis*. This is clear when we consider the nature of Christian existence in the world. Just as the universalistic motif compels the church to adopt a radical stance *for* the world, so the dualistic motif causes the church to do battle *against* the world—all the more so because the cross of Christ represents God's radical "No" to the value structures of our present world. For the powers of this age have not only crucified Christ (1 Cor. 2:8) but continue to crucify those who belong to Christ (2 Cor. 4:7-12). The church is the sign of the dawning of the new age in the midst of the old, and thus the vanguard of God's new world, battling against the forces of evil and being beleaguered by them. Paul expresses this theme of the church *over against* the world in several ways: it is the battle of the Spirit against the flesh (Gal. 5:17); of faith in Christ against the dominion of the Law (Gal. 2:15-21); of the foolishness of the cross over against the wisdom of the world (1 Cor. 1:18-25); yes, ultimately, of the powers of life over against the powers of death (Rom. 8:38-39).

In the midst of this battle, there is *necessary suffering*: not only suffering to be endured passively because of the onslaught of the powers of this world but also suffering as a result of active engagement with the world because the church has a redemptive mission in the world for the world in accordance with the redemptive plan of God.

The church, then, lives in continuous tension between being *against the world* and being *for the world*. If it emphasizes too strongly withdrawal from the world in a dualistic fashion, it threatens to become a purely sectarian apocalyptic movement that betrays the death and resurrection of Christ as God's redemptive plan for the world; but if it exclusively emphasizes participation in the world, it threatens to become another "worldly" phenomenon, accommodating itself to whatever the world will buy and so becoming a part of the world.

There is however a suprapersonal or cosmic dimension to the historical suffering of the church. Ephesians expresses it well:

For we are not contending against flesh and blood, but against the principalities, against the powers, against the world rulers of this present darkness, against the spiritual hosts of wickedness in the heavenly places (Eph. 6:12).

Although Paul, unlike Ephesians, rarely enumerates the transcendent inhabitants of the heavenly world, it is clear that he shares the apocalyptic sentiment of Ephesians: behind the manifestations of human sins lies a field of organized evil, summarized by Paul as the powers of "the flesh," "the Law," "sin," and "death." This field operates as an interrelated whole; it is an alliance of powers under the sovereign and cosmic rule of death. Death is indeed "the last enemy" (1 Cor. 15:26), and until it has been destroyed the completed victory of God's rule cannot be asserted. And so the reign of death in the world intensifies the suffering of the church. For although Christians participate in the dominion of Christ who in his resurrection has overcome death (Rom. 6:9), and although they are people "who have been brought from death to life" (Rom. 6:13), death is still the signature of existence for both the church and the world. Christians are still subject to death (1 Thess. 4:13) and death still manifests itself in creation's "bondage to decay" (Rom. 8:21) and "futility" (Rom. 8:20), that is, in all "the slings and arrows of outrageous fortune," in all the groanings and sufferings that pervade this world.

For Paul, as for Jewish apocalyptic, suffering is caused by sin, especially by the sin of Adam, which unleashed death into the world:

Therefore as sin came into the world through one man and death through sin, and so death spread to all men because all men sinned (Rom. 5:12).

The causal relationship between sin and death, which he affirms along with Jewish apocalyptic, involves Paul, so it seems to me, in a contradiction about Christian *suffering* in the world.

If sin and death are causally related, then it follows that the *defeat of sin* by Jesus Christ entails as well the *defeat of death*.

(1) Paul now asserts that Christians indeed participate in Christ's victory over *sin* so that henceforth the power of sin is no longer operative in the church as the domain of Christ (Rom. 6:1-23).

(2) According to Paul, Christians also participate in Christ's victory over *death* (Rom. 6:9) in some sense. They are people "who have been brought from death to life" (Rom. 6:13), although Paul states elsewhere that death remains "the last enemy" (1 Cor. 15:26).

(3) Why then, we must ask, are Christians still subject to death? If Christ has overcome sin, the causal agent of death, how can Paul claim that sin, but not death, has been eradicated for Christians? In other words, how can Paul simultaneously conjoin and disjoin the powers of sin and death? On the one hand, he claims that sin and death are so intimately related that the presence and absence of the one signifies the presence and absence of the other (Rom. 5:12). But on the other hand, he claims that the power of sin *has been* defeated by Christ, whereas the power of death is *still* a present power in Christian life and so causes Christians to suffer and die.

(4) This contradiction in Paul occurs because he is unwilling to state what *we must assert*: that sin and death are in some sense independent agents because the sufferings caused by sin and those caused by death cannot be fully equated in human experience.

There is much suffering in the world, seemingly meaningless precisely because it cannot be reduced to human sin.

(5) Therefore, because Paul denies with Jewish apocalyptic that sin and death are to some extent independent agents, he involves himself in a necessary contradiction when he addresses the question of why Christians suffer in the world. His answer is actually twofold: (a) Christians suffer because of the onslaught of *the power of sin* in the world. Just because the Christian community is free from the power of sin, sin continuously attempts to get a foothold in the church and its members. (b) Christians also suffer because of *the presence of death* in the world—a

presence which is partially related to sin but which is also (even more so?) related to our life in a creation that is subject to decay and futility and in which Christians and non-Christians alike participate.

Thus, according to Paul, Christians *have been* set free from the power of sin and *will be* set free from the power of death, once death, "the last enemy" (1 Cor. 15:26), will have been defeated in the final triumph of God.

In other words, although Paul claims with Jewish apocalyptic that death, and thus suffering, is to be attributed to sin, he in fact leaves room for the thought that there is a crucial and mysterious "dark" residue of evil and death in God's created order. This evil residue—of evil and death—that cannot be attributed to human sin causes suffering and will be removed only at the hour of God's final triumph.

The motif of dualism then stresses that God's plan *for* the world engages the Christians in a battle *against* the present structures of the world. It points to the reality that God's victory in Christ motivates Christians to a hope that incarnates itself in a cruciform existence, that is, in a life under the cross.

Imminence

The apocalyptic motif of imminence or the impending actualization of God's reign is closely related to the three motifs discussed above. It intensifies the others and thus heightens the hope for the actualization of God's vindication and universal reign, whereas it hopes as well for the elimination of all dualistic structures and their concomitant suffering.

The motif of imminence is a troublesome one. In fact, it comes as no surprise that it leads us to a fundamental difficulty with Paul's apocalyptic gospel. After all, how can we maintain an attitude of hope in an *imminent* arrival of the kingdom of God in the face of the sheer continuation of chronological time? Has Paul's expectation of the impending nearness of the kingdom of God not been refuted by the historical process itself, and does not continuing adherence to such an expectation simply mean a false hope?

Indeed, although scholars usually concede that apocalyptic terminology is an important building block in Paul's theology, its futurist-imminent aspect represents an obstacle to our modern mentality, to the extent that it is either demythologized in an existentialist fashion or neutralized.*

Here, if anywhere, the interpretive tension between "what it meant" and "what it means" is obvious. The so-called primitive world view of apocalyptic and the delay of the parousia are, for most modern interpreters, such an overwhelming problem, and the utopian distortions and delusions of apocalyptic fanatics such an embarrassment, that Paul's emphasis on the imminent parousia is for all practical purposes either treated as peripheral, or existentially reinterpreted, or subjected to development theories. It is either characterized as a flexible variable over against the constant of the Christ-event as the center of Paul's thought, or it is considered to be an option of the early Paul which he abandoned in his mature years (see chapter 6, below), or it is simply called a mistaken notion of Paul. I will address this important issue later on (see chapters 7 and 8, below) but must first of all delineate the meaning of the imminence motif for Paul himself.

There are at least three aspects to the theme of imminence in Paul: (1) its necessity, (2) its incalculability, and (3) the dialectic of patience and impatience.

(1) *Necessity.* The expectation of the imminent parousia of Christ and the day of the Lord is for Paul not an apocalyptic oddity but the climax of his theological fabric. William Wrede's comments of 1904 are still very much to the point:

---

*It is interesting, for example, that Rudolf Bultmann readily adopts the motifs of universalism and dualism because they can easily be accommodated in his existentialist program as *Entweltlichung* (desecularization), whereas the motif of imminence is for him an obsolete apocalyptic remnant in Paul's thought that Paul himself had already commenced to demythologize.

The whole Pauline conception of salvation is characterized by suspense which strains forward toward the final release, the actual death. . . . In this connection we should keep before our minds with especial clearness a fact which, indeed, when we are dealing with Paul, ought never to be forgotten. He believed with all his might in the speedy coming of Christ and the approaching end of the world. In consequence, the redemptive act of Christ, which lay in the past, and the dawn of the future glory lay in his view, close together. . . . It has been popularly held that Paul departed from the view of salvation of the early Church by shifting the stress from the future to the past, looking upon the blessedness of the Christian as already attained, and emphasizing faith instead of hope. It is easy to see that this is assuredly but a half truth. All references to the redemption as a completed transaction swing around at once into utterances about the future. . . . There are deep-reaching differences between the Pauline doctrine of redemption and the thoughts of modern belief.[4]

The impending return of Christ is made necessary by Paul's conviction about the resurrection of Jesus Christ. Resurrection language *is* apocalyptic language: it receives its meaning from the apocalyptic hope in the resurrection of the dead, which will take place when all history finds its fulfillment in the manifestation of the apocalyptic glory of God. When Paul designates Christ as "the first fruits" of the final resurrection of the dead (1 Cor. 15:20, 23) or as the "firstborn among many brethren to come" (Rom. 8:29), he proclaims the *necessary* connection between the resurrection of Christ and the final resurrection of the dead. Thus the Christ-event is not a closure—or completed event. As "first fruits" it strains toward its actualization in the harvest of the final resurrection of the dead. The resurrection of Christ can bear no other meaning than its *anticipatory* significance for the future resurrection of the dead. The necessary connection between Christ and the future triumph of God is confirmed by Paul's view of the Spirit. The Spirit is related to the future glory of God in the same manner that Christ is related to the future resurrection of the dead. In fact, the Spirit is the agent of the future glory in the present; it is the first down payment or guarantee of the end-time (Rom. 8:23; 2 Cor. 1:22) and thus the signal of its coming. It is therefore no surprise that both military and promissory images convey the Spirit's activity. As the vanguard of the kingdom's power, it battles the power of the flesh and in doing so moves people into the direction of the future from which the Spirit comes, that is, the future of God's glory.

Moreover, the coming of Christ is eagerly expected because there is an existential contradiction between empirical existence in the world and the promise of the resurrection of Christ.

The cry of the martyrs under the altar in Revelation, "O Sovereign Lord, holy and true, how long before thou wilt judge and avenge our blood on those who dwell upon the earth" (Rev. 6:10) echoes in many ways the one of the members of the Pauline churches—"Maranatha"—"Our Lord, come" (1 Cor. 16:22)—especially when they remember Paul's interpretation of the Eucharist: "For as often as you eat this bread and drink the cup, you proclaim the Lord's death until he comes" (1 Cor. 11:26). And so Paul exhorts his Philippians: "Rejoice in the Lord always; again I will say, Rejoice. Let all men know your forbearance. The Lord is at hand" (Phil. 4:4–5) and "I am sure that he who began a good work in you will bring it to completion at the day of Jesus Christ" (Phil. 1:6).

The imminence motif in Paul's letters, then, is even more intense than in Jewish apocalyptic: it is intensified by the death and resurrection of Christ because that event marks the incursion of the future into the present. Christ who has come in the fullness of time (Gal. 4:4) has inaugurated the end *of* time so that no eschatological timetable needs to be established, and in principle no other conditions need to be met before his glorious return in the triumph of God.

And so the apocalyptic motifs of vindication, universalism, and dualism are all embraced by the intensity of the hope in the universal and cosmic reign of God that will resolve all dualistic structures of the present and all suffering. The antiphony of

Revelation 22 might as well have been taken out of the liturgy of a Pauline church:

> The Spirit and the Bride say, "Come."
> And let him who hears say, "Come" (v. 17).
> "Surely I am coming soon."
> Amen. Come, Lord Jesus! (v. 20).

Indeed, at that time Paul's hope will be actualized:

> I consider that the sufferings of this present time are not worth comparing with the glory that is to be revealed to us (Rom. 8:18).

(2) *Incalculability.* Without hope in the imminent coming of God and of Christ as the definitive closure—or completion—event of history, there can be no authentic Pauline theology. But we must remember as well that Paul's apocalyptic becomes distorted when that hope becomes the object of human calculation, speculation, and prediction. Paul's Christian hope is a matter of prophecy, not a matter of prediction. The incalculability of this hope is for Paul one of its essential marks. Thus the apocalyptic program of 2 Thessalonians 2 is so unlike anything in Paul's authentic letters that many scholars have ascribed that letter to a non-Pauline author. Indeed, 2 Thessalonians 2 has more in common with the synoptic apocalypses (Mark 13; Luke 17, 21; Matt. 24) and the book of Revelation (see p. 98) than with the authentic letters of Paul. After all, Paul is a writer of letters and not of apocalypses; he uses apocalyptic motifs but not the literary genre of apocalypse. Whereas the apocalyptic composition often concentrates on a timetable of events or on a program for the sake of calculating apocalyptic events, Paul stresses to the contrary the incalculability of the end. Instead of narrating apocalyptic events in a temporal sequence of "first," "unless," "then," Paul emphasizes the unexpected, the suddenness and surprising character of the final theophany (1 Thess. 5:2-10). Moreover, the incalculable character of the end motivates Paul to restrain severely his use of apocalyptic language and imagery. In fact, Paul's theology is often characterized as

nonapocalyptic because, contrary to Revelation, he lacks interest in heavenly topography and in portraying the scenes of the last judgment or those of the heavenly kingdom. But this feature of his theology is directly related to the radical character of his imminent expectation. For how can he be engaged in a philosophy of history or in a predictive eschatology when there is only one stance possible, that is, the stance of living within the time of the end, when the risen Christ is about to complete what God has inaugurated through him at the time of his death and resurrection? For those "upon whom the end of the ages has come" (1 Cor. 10:1), for those who participate in the powers of the dawning new age, what else can their attitude be but rejoicing in "the God of hope . . . with all joy and peace" (Rom. 15:13)?

Paul—the prophet of God's glory—does not deduce from a variety of historical events the date of God's coming reign; rather he deduces from God's promises, confirmed by Christ, the impending nearness of the vindication of these promises. The imminence of God's universal rule, then, is grounded in a radical faith in and openness to the God of the promise and not in a historical determinism, as if the believer can live by speculative knowledge rather than by faith.

Thus the delay of the parousia is not a theological concern for Paul. It is not an embarrassment for him; it does not compel him to shift the center of his attention from apocalyptic imminence to a form of "realized eschatology," that is to a conviction of the full presence of the kingdom of God in our present history. It is of the essence of his faith in Christ that adjustments in his expectations can occur without a surrender of these expectations (1 Thess. 4:13–18; 1 Cor. 15:15–51; 2 Cor. 5:1–10; Phil. 2:21–24). Indeed, the hope in God's imminent rule through Christ remains the constant in his letters from beginning to end, that is, from 1 Thessalonians to Philippians and Romans.

At this point the reader may ask: "Why do you call Paul an apocalyptic theologian, if in fact *his* hope in the imminent arrival of the kingdom of God contradicts the usual Jewish—and Christian—apocalyptic portrayals of imminence? Moreover, can you really maintain that Paul does not in the apocalyptic manner project a sequence of apocalyptic events to come?''

My response to this dual question is as follows: first, I designate the imminence motif in Paul as apocalyptic only in the sense that, with the apocalyptic authors, Paul expects the future to entail a definitive closure/completion-event in time and space, rather than simply a continuous, open-ended process. My characterization of Paul as an apocalyptic theologian, then, contains a polemical edge against those interpreters who exchange the specificity of the end-time for a philosophical argument about God as futurity, that is, as "always One who comes."[5] Moreover, the term "future apocalyptic" guards against the multivalent and often chaotic use of the concept "eschatology" in modern theology. John Macquarrie makes this clear when in discussing the doctrine of the *eschata* or "last things" he remarks:

> Immediately, of course, an ambiguity discloses itself. The "last things" may be the things that come along at the end of a series, and here "last" has primarily a temporal significance. Yet—the "last things" may also be understood as what is final and ultimate, what is of most importance; and in some modern theologians (Bultmann and Tillich are examples) the eschatological is virtually voided of any temporal reference and is understood as the ultimate or decisive moment.[6]

Second, I stated earlier (see p. 47): "Christ, who has come in the fullness of time" (Gal. 4:4) "has inaugurated the end *of* time, so that . . . in principle no other conditions need to be met before his glorious return in the triumph of God." This statement needs to be qualified in the light of Paul's occasional speech about a special end-time revelation (*mysterion*) which he has received (Rom. 11:25; 1 Cor. 15:51) and in the light of his expectation that certain events will take place before the end in a certain sequence. Thus Paul expects "the full number of the Gentiles" to come in before the partial hardening of Israel is lifted

(Rom. 11:25). In 1 Cor. 15:23, he speaks about the "order" of apocalyptic events (see also 1 Cor. 15:51-52) and in 1 Thess. 4:13-18 about a preference of the dead over the living at the time of the parousia. However, it is remarkable that Paul rarely speaks this way and that most often an ethical or specific theological concern overshadows the predictive elements. In Romans 11 Paul needs to confirm the theological motif of Israel's eschatological destiny for the sake of God's continuing faithfulness to Israel. In 1 Thessalonians 4 he needs to comfort those who mourn over the dead and are misinformed about their status in God's kingdom. In 1 Corinthians 15 he needs to counter a realized eschatology by emphasizing the distinction between the reign of Christ and the reign of God. In short, the necessity of the impending end of history and its incalculability do not suspend each other, as if the one neutralizes the other. Rather they are conjoined in Paul, because when the intensity of the hope collapses into its predictability, the character of Christian faith as absolute dependence on the God of the promises is distorted.

And as I will argue in the next section, the dialectic of patience and impatience in Paul's apostolic life confirms the dynamic tension between the necessity and the incalculability of the imminence motif.

(3) *Patience/impatience.* The dialectic of patience and impatience in Paul's apostolic life seems at first glance to be an outright contradiction. For how is it possible for Paul to be engaged in two seemingly opposite activities? How can he simultaneously long for the future reign of God and yet be occupied with missionary strategy for the long run? How do this impatience and this patience cohere in his life? In the light of what we know about apocalyptic sects, would we not expect an otherworldly attitude, accompanied by ethical passivity, in the knowledge that "the appointed time has grown very short" (1 Cor. 7:29) and that "the form of this world is passing away" (1 Cor. 7:31)? If the conviction of the *necessity* of the imminent end compels Paul to a passionate disengagement with the structures

of this world (1 Cor. 7:29-31) and to an ecstatic anticipation of the coming glory of God (1 Cor. 14:18; 2 Cor. 12:12; cf. 2 Cor. 12:1-7a), how can such passionate anticipation be correlated with Paul's insistence on sobriety (2 Cor. 5:13) and endurance (Rom. 8:25) and with his pragmatic pastoral care and anxiety for the well-being and outreach of his churches (2 Cor. 11:28)? In other words, how are passion and sobriety related in his personal life, and how are apostolicity and apocalyptic related in his missionary activity?

Passion and sobriety go hand in hand in Paul's life because the necessity of the imminent end is directly related to its incalculability. This gives Paul the freedom to be committed simultaneously to the imminence of the end and to the contingencies of historical circumstance. He who has seen the signs of the coming transformation of the world in the story of Jesus Christ and has seen its consequences for the church is able to allow God the freedom to choose the moment of his final glorious theophany, whereas he strains in the meantime to move God's world into the direction of its appointed future destiny. There is passion in Paul—but it is the passion of sobriety; and there is impatience in Paul—but it is impatience tempered by the patience of preparing the world for its coming destiny, which the Christ-event has inaugurated.

There is, then, no conflict between apostolicity and apocalyptic in Paul: apocalyptic fervor and missionary strategy go hand in hand. Paul is simply not an apocalyptic fanatic who runs breathlessly through the Roman Empire because the end of the world is imminent. He spends, for instance, one and a half years at Corinth and three years at Ephesus and contemplates a mission to Spain (Rom. 15:24). And so eschatology and missionary strategy do not contradict each other, as if the one paralyzes the strength of the other. The mission charge in Acts 1:6-8 is much more concerned with the alternative—eschatology or missions—than anything in Paul. Paul can contemplate a universal mission and yet think in terms of apocalyptic imminence. The success of a universal mission is never posited as the precondition for the end—something which Acts 1:8 alludes to with its missionary charge "to the end of the earth" and which Mark 13:10 affirms unequivocally: "But the gospel must first be preached to all nations." It is only in Col. 1:21–29 and in Eph. 3:1–13, the deutero-Pauline letters, that Paul is portrayed as the minister of a universal gospel to the Gentiles in such a manner that his mission is not balanced by apocalyptic intensity.

Impatience and patience, then, do not neutralize each other in Paul's ministry (apostolate) but seem to reinforce each other. Hope is for Paul accompanied by both impatient fervor and patient strategies. In order to understand this central aspect of Paul's theology more adequately, I intend to explore the central affirmation of Paul's apostolate and thought, that is, the existential and ethical dimension of his apocalyptic gospel.

4

Apocalyptic and Ministry

I have argued that Paul's gospel is dominated by four basic Jewish apocalyptic motifs: vindication, universalism, dualism, and imminence. Paul radically modifies and restructures these motifs because of God's saving intervention in the death and resurrection of Jesus Christ: they have, as it were, been baptized into Christ with the result that these motifs now function in a new setting. Yet, however modified and restructured, the mutual interaction and interpenetration of these motifs constitute the center of Paul's thought and determine his manner of interpreting it for the sake of Christian visibility in the world. Paul's thought and method, therefore, are not to be divorced from each other. His gospel is precisely gospel and not a structure of abstract thought because thought and method are reciprocally related and do not exist apart from each other. Thought gives rise to practice and practice gives rise to thought, and Paul's manner of interpretation conjoins both. Paul's gospel is neither a structure of abstract thought nor simply an ever-shifting variable that lives off the opportunism of the moment and that changes the content of the gospel according to the needs of the marketplace. I call this correlation of thought and practice the reciprocal relationship of coherence and contingency—a relationship that resembles the theological method of Third World theologians. It is a method that bases theological reflection on the concrete situations of the church in society.

The relation between coherence and contingency is important because it explains Paul's central method of doing theology. It means that Paul's way of interpreting the gospel moves between two foci: the *abiding core* of the gospel, which does not accommodate itself to the various tastes of the times, and the *variables* of historical situations to which the gospel addresses itself so that its word becomes a word on target. The interface between coherence and contingency, then, expresses the incarnational or this-worldly thrust of Paul's apocalyptic gospel. Paul's apocalyptic gospel has indeed an abiding center of truth (Gal. 2:5, 14), but that truth is only then authentic if it addresses itself to the particularity of the human contexts that the gospel must address with its promise of God's coming reign. And so the truth of the gospel is not a theoretically frozen proposition that demands a subsequent and secondary practical and casuistic application to a variety of human situations. Therefore, Paul is not engaged in simply imposing the objective content of the gospel on his various audiences, as if his preaching amounts to a monotonous repetition of "Pauline doctrine." The opposite is also not true. Paul does not accommodate the gospel to "what the market will buy," as if the integrity of the gospel can be surrendered to an incoherent display of incidental, opportunistic, and compromising thoughts that vary from situation to situation.

Moreover, the reciprocal relation between the coherent center of Paul's gospel and its contingent interpretation means that the content of Paul's gospel cannot be grasped by simply selecting one of the key terms which make up his gospel. Key terms like the righteousness of God, justification, redemption, or reconciliation are not to be measured over against each other as if one term is *the* permanent key to which all others are subservient. Rather these several key terms are metaphors that must convey the gospel to a particular situation in accordance with their appropriateness to that situation.

The coherence of Paul's gospel, then, is not constituted by a specific formula or concept. Rather, we must think of that coherence in terms of a *field of meaning* determined by the apocalyptic setting of God's act in the death and resurrection of

Christ. The field of meaning comprises the apocalyptic motifs (which I discussed above), as restructured by the Christ-event. The field of meaning, then, originates in the primordial or original experience of Paul's apostolic call. It is the product of Paul's interpretation of Christ's appearance to him. Paul therefore interprets the Christ-event in the framework of his apocalyptic religious language, which was the language of both his Pharisaic past and of the early Christians before him. And Paul's apostolic call was for him a call to missionize the Gentile world (Gal. 1:15-16) in order to prepare the world for God's coming glory. The Christophany then is interpreted by Paul in terms of his prior apocalyptic convictions, and it both modifies and intensifies those convictions radically. It signifies for him primarily the inauguration of the reign of God, which according to God's purpose must embrace his whole creation, that is, both Jews and Gentiles, and for which Paul must prepare the way.

An important clue, however, to Paul's apostolic mission is the correlation of apocalyptic and apostolate in his life. That correlation is determined by the fact that the apocalyptic *purpose* of God's redemptive will is inseparable from the *manner* of its execution. Because the *manner* of God's coming apocalyptic triumph is made manifest in the death and resurrection of Christ, the apostle must therefore communicate in his own apostolic life both the *purpose* of God's intervention in Christ and its *manner*.

Thus apocalyptic and apostolate are deeply intertwined. The relation between the coherent core of the gospel and its contingent interpretation expresses that correlation. The apostle is not charged with simply pronouncing the end of the world to the world. Rather that charge must be executed in the context of enlarging in this world the domain of God's coming world because God's coming world envisages the transformation of the world's present structures and not simply their dissolution. And because Christ and the Spirit are the first manifestations of this transformation, the apostle must prepare the world for the manner and goal of God's redemptive plan.

Therefore the manner of Paul's apostolate is the manner of

both the incarnation and the death and resurrection of Jesus Christ. Or to state it differently: the future apocalyptic vision manifests itself as a this-worldly and cruciform activity. The apostle has gained a clarity of vision that enables him to detect the signs of God's coming triumph within the structures of this world. Those signs are the signs of both God's judgment and his love and righteousness that embrace the sin and suffering of people in our present world and grant them newness of life, courage and hope. And because our world is marked by an enormous diversity of people, all with their special psychological, socioeconomic, and cultural conditions, the manner of preaching the apocalyptic gospel must be one of flexibility, sensitivity, and empathy. For unless the apocalyptic word of the gospel is a word on target, it bypasses its christological shape and becomes merely an apocalyptic blast that encourages all the sins of the religious world of humankind, such as secret knowledge about the future, ethical passivity, disdain for God's world, and the elitism of the in-group.

The interplay, then, between coherence and contingency accords with the apocalyptic intensity of Paul's gospel. A Pauline apocalyptic knows that God's final triumph is already casting its rays into our present world, however opaque these rays often are and however much they seem contradicted by the empirical reality of our present world. The point is that the present time is not *set over against* the future reign of God as if the future reign of God will be nothing but a compensation for his present absence. Rather, the interim time between the Christ-event and the visible manifestation of the reign of God is a time in which the presence of the crucified and risen Christ prepares for his future return in glory. Paul's apocalyptic envisions God as the coming one who has already come to his creation in Christ and who already gathers people into his kingdom by revealing his presence to them through the power of the Word and the Spirit. In other words, the coherent center of the gospel implies in a most direct manner its contingent power and effectiveness. ''For you know how, like a father with his children, we exhorted each one of you and encouraged you and charged you to lead a life worthy of God, who calls you into his own kingdom and glory" (1 Thess. 2:11-12). Indeed, "He who calls you is faithful, and he will do it" (1 Thess. 5:24). God the faithful one has already come in Christ and is continuously preparing for his final coming through the contingent message and effectiveness of the gospel.

5

Apocalyptic: A Misreading of Paul's Gospel?

By and large the future apocalyptic dimension of Paul's thought has been misinterpreted in the history of the church. The interpretation of futurist eschatology in the church has been one long process of its transposition into a different key. Especially under the influence of Origen and Augustine future eschatology was made to refer either to the spiritual journey of the believer or to the church as the kingdom of God on earth.

From the condemnation of the prophetic movement of Montanism in the second century A.D. and the exclusion of millennial apocalyptic at the Council of Ephesus (A.D. 431) through its condemnation by the Reformers (in the Augsburg Confession) and until today, future eschatology was pushed out of the mainstream of church life and thus relegated to the ranks of heretical aberrations. The impact of this spiritualizing process and the distaste for the apocalyptic speculations of sectarian groups have no doubt contributed to the overwhelmingly negative estimate of apocalyptic by biblical and theological scholarship since the Enlightenment of the eighteenth century.

Already in the nineteenth century apocalyptic had been removed from Paul's thought as an ornamental husk. This was followed in our time by the demythologizing program of Rudolf Bultmann, who translated Paul's apocalyptic into existentialist categories, that is, as directed to the authentic existence of persons.

And so it comes as no surprise that Neo-orthodoxy collapsed apocalyptic into Christology: "eschatological" not only displaced the "bad" term "apocalyptic" but was stripped as well of its temporal reference and was now understood as "ultimate" (see p. 50, above).

Other solutions to the future apocalyptic "embarrassment" of Paul were proposed by various scholars such as C.H. Dodd and Oscar Cullmann. C.H. Dodd located the center of Paul's thought in "realized eschatology" (see p. 66, below), whereas Oscar Cullman construed that thought in terms of "salvation-history" (see p. 74, below). Indeed, as James M. Robinson has remarked, our prevalent way of overcoming the difficulty of Paul's apocalyptic seems to lie either in the solution of realized eschatology or in that of salvation-history. [1]*

In recent decades, however, there has been a decisive shift in the history of Pauline interpretation. Preceded by scholars like Johannes Weiss and Albert Schweitzer, many biblical scholars have drawn renewed attention to apocalyptic in Paul and so

---

*Ernst Käsemann seems to be on target in his comments on the history of research:

The history of the theology of the last two generations shows that the rediscovery of primitive Christian apocalyptic in its significance for the New Testament, for which we are indebted especially to Kabisch, Johannes Weiss and Albert Schweitzer, provided discoverers and contemporaries alike with such a shock as we are hardly able to imagine. Weiss retreated with all speed into the liberal conception of Jesus, Schweitzer proceeded boldly to draw the logical consequences from his theses about the historical Jesus—which, to make things worse, were themselves untenable—and, for the rest, there was zealous study of the realms of the comparative study of religions, of cultic devotion and of mysticism. Barth's *Epistle to the Romans* brought "thoroughgoing eschatology" back out of its existence among the shades and made it into the keynote of New Testament interpretation in Germany, of course in a multiplicity of very disparate versions. The general trend is admittedly in the same direction and can hardly be summed up better than by a quotation from P. Althaus, *Die Letzten Dinge, Lehrbuch der Eschatologie,* 7th ed., 1957, p. 272: "In principle the world comes to an end with the judgment, with the kingdom, with Christ. In this sense every historical time, like history in its totality, is the time of the End, because individually and as a totality these times lap like waves on the shores of eternity, each exposed directly to its judgment and its redemption. To this extent all the hours in history are one and the same last hour." It is the achievement of M. Werner in his controversial book *Die Entstehung des christlichen Dogmas,* 1941 (ET, *The Formation of Christian Dogma,* 1957) that he recalled us to the unsettled problem, more or less industriously eliminated or pushed away to the outer fringe of our awareness, of primitive Christian apocalyptic, although it is true that he failed to get New Testament scholars in any respect beyond the theses of Schweitzer.

have systematic theologians like Jürgen Moltmann and Wolf-hart Pannenberg (see p. 102, below). In particular, Ernst Käse-mann must be given credit for the vigorous advocacy of his thesis that apocalyptic was "the mother of Christian theology."[2] However, because I will focus on the challenge of Paul's apoc-alyptic for the church today, my concern is not only with the *historical* assessment of Paul's apocalyptic, that is, the question of "what it meant," but also with its enduring theological sig-nificance, that is, with "what it means." In other words, the re-lation of the descriptive-historical to the normative assessment of Paul's apocalyptic is at stake.

It is interesting that scholars who emphasize apocalyptic as the key to a *historical* description of Paul's thought rarely posit that key as a relevant possibility for the church today. They either retreat into some developmental scheme (for instance, Joseph A. Fitzmyer)[3] or stay within the historical boundaries of their investigation. Ernst Käsemann is a prime example of this latter tendency. His assertion about apocalyptic as the mother of Christian theology is not followed by a hermeneutical trans-fer of apocalyptic to the present—something he engages in eagerly when treating topics such as justification by faith.

In other words, the disjunction between "what it meant" and "what it means" is particularly acute in the apocalyptic inter-preters of Paul—not least because of the embarrassment caused by the twin features of the delay of the parousia and the primi-tive world view of apocalyptic. E. P. Sanders, for instance, re-marks on the difficulty of finding a category that enables us moderns to grasp Paul's notion of participation in Christ:

> To an appreciable degree, what Paul concretely thought cannot be directly appropriated by Christians today. The form of the present world did not pass away, the end did not come and be-lievers were not caught up to meet the Lord in the heavens. *Paul did express himself in terms which have proved more durable, and it is reasonable that those who wish to make Paul's gospel relevant today should emphasize them* [italics mine].[4]

And James M. Robinson states:

> An imminent expectation can no longer be fulfilled, since our
> time is no longer near to that time. But all other modifications
> of the time pattern are equally unfulfillable. Anyone who would
> try to claim that God's reign has already come, that is, that our
> world is the kingdom of God deserves to be laughed or cried
> down. But he who seeks a position between those extremes—is
> also refuted by the non-fulfillment of the consummation. For a
> thinking person today all temporal alternatives are equally in-
> valid.[5]

NONAPOCALYPTIC INTERPRETERS
OF PAUL

Unlike the apocalyptic interpreters of Paul's gospel, the nonapocalyptic interpreters to be discussed here are much more interested in bridging the gap between "what it meant" and "what
it means." Although they argue a nonapocalyptic presentation
of Paul on strictly historical grounds, their particular historical
convictions enable them to suggest the permanent relevance of
Paul for today.

It is certainly the task of every interpreter to bridge the gap
between "what it meant" and "what it means." This is true because the process of understanding is basically a unified process
in which historical and theological understandings ultimately
fuse. Therefore we cannot separate historical and theological
judgments in watertight compartments. The attainment of a
purely "objective" interpretation is an unrealistic objective because, notwithstanding our duty to attend to the particularities
of historical truth, the historicity of the interpreters themselves
necessarily influences their perspectives on the material. We
should note that for the nonapocalyptic interpreters of Paul the
gap between past and present can be closed more readily because they do not consider apocalyptic to be an interpretive key
to the historical Paul. Since I will attempt to refute their proposals on historical grounds, the question of the normative character of Paul's apocalyptic gospel for us needs to be faced with

a new urgency. For how can the gap between past and present be bridged if apocalyptic is indeed the key to Paul's thought? And if that gap cannot be bridged, will I not be compelled to admit that the apocalyptic of the historical Paul needs a radical reinterpretation for our time?

But if this should be the case, how is it then possible to maintain the integrity of Paul's gospel? If Paul is indeed an apocalyptic theologian, and if our post-Enlightenment world view deems his apocalyptic to be an impossible option for the church today, how does this affect the total structure of Paul's gospel? If we cannot maintain the apocalyptic of Paul as the crucial ingredient of his gospel, are we then forced to live with an abbreviated gospel, that is, with a gospel that even in its central core is subject to the contingencies and fluctuations of history?

The issue under discussion, then, is twofold: Is the center of Paul's thought indeed to be located in his christologically determined future apocalyptic? And if this can be affirmed, is this apocalyptic gospel still a relevant gospel for our time?

I will now discuss the theories of those scholars who refute the claim of an "apocalyptic" Paul and opt for a nonapocalyptic interpretation of Paul on historical grounds. Subsequently I will address the question of the relevance of Paul's gospel for our time (see chapters 6 and 7, below).

The nonapocalyptic interpreters of Paul can be classified into three basic schools of thought: the solution of *realized eschatology,* the *existentialist analysis* of the gospel, the scheme of *salvation-history.* In every case these scholars see Paul engaged in a radical reinterpretation of the apocalyptic traditions that he inherited from the early church.

This applies especially to the saving events of the death and resurrection of Christ: the nonapocalyptic interpreters have a specific view not only of the relation between the death and resurrection of Christ but also of its saving effects on believers.

Some locate the center of Paul's thought exclusively in the cross of Christ and in a cruciform life for believers—which they often interpret in terms of the "paradox" of salvation.* This view regards the resurrection of Christ chiefly as the interpretive key of the cross and subsumes the resurrection under the cross.

Others assign to the resurrection a more distinct and independent significance in its relation to the cross: the reality of the resurrection actualizes itself here in the church as the body of Christ so that Paul's thought climaxes in his doctrine of the church, that is, in the worldwide mission of the divine commonwealth.

Still others locate the center of Paul's thought in the axis of the Christ-event and the future eschatological consummation, which they often clarify with the image of the relation of D-Day to V-Day. Here the abiding core of Paul's thought is located in the Christ-event as the center of time, enabling Paul (and other New Testament authors) to render the eschatological consummation as a shifting variable that in no way affects the christological center.

The solution of realized eschatology as the center of Paul's thought is represented by C. H. Dodd and his followers.[6] Dodd argues that Paul's early career is marked by an apocalyptic structure of thought (1 Thessalonians) that he gradually abandoned because of his growing insight into the meaning of the Christ-event as the "realization" of the kingdom of God in history and because of the obstacles future apocalyptic produced for Paul's Gentile mission. The stage of Paul's maturity is reached in Ephesians where the apocalyptic consummation of history is displaced by the church as the divine commonwealth on earth.

The proponents of realized eschatology operate with two basic interpretive keys: (1) a developmental psychological scheme, which can be traced throughout the letters of Paul; and (2) a substitution of the doctrine of the church for apocalyptic, that is, a gradual shift in Paul from eschatology to ecclesiology.

---

*These interpreters also use the term "salvation '*sub contrario,*' " by which they mean: the gift of salvation in a way that seems to be its opposite from an empirical point of view (for instance, salvation as life under the cross).

(1) The psychological approach is indeed able to do justice to the various patterns of Paul's thought, and thus it liberates the religious person of Paul from sterile and rigid dogmatic categories. The fatal flaw of the method lies in the developmental scheme and the assumption of a demonstrable evolutionary process in Paul. It not only assumes the authenticity of the deutero-Pauline letters, Colossians and Ephesians, in order to prove or at least strengthen its case for Paul's mature thought on the doctrine of the church—a doctrine that is indeed the mark of these letters—but also posits a psychological development in Paul which supposedly has access to Paul's pretextual psyche. The center of Paul's thought is thus located in the developing stages of his personality. Recently this approach has gained new strength in the debate about the shifting trends in the letters of Paul. Thus Gerd Lüdemann is engaged in a three-volume work on Paul, of which the first volume investigates Pauline chronology.[7] The chronology must prepare the way for a delineation of the changes in Paul's thought that occur, for example, between 1 Thessalonians and 1 Corinthians.

What is at stake here is whether Paul's apocalyptic is the stable center of his thought. My apocalyptic proposal does not imply, however, that Paul never changed his mind but rather explores the *weight* and *quality* of these changes. Unless one is committed to a rigid Pauline dogmatism, one cannot deny that a man shifts his thoughts on particular subjects during his lifetime. And so the notion of change is welcome because it does justice to the dynamic and flexible character of Paul's thought. I maintain, for example, that contingent situations in the mission churches compel Paul to render the gospel in different ways and with different emphases according to the need of the hour (see chapter 4, above). Moreover, it can be demonstrated that Paul changed his mind about issues like the date of the parousia, his own participation in it before his death, or the precise status of the dead before the parousia. It seems clear that—at least prior to 1 Thessalonians—the status of the dead in Christ had not been central to Paul's founding message in Thessalonica or (what is more likely) had not been properly understood (1 Thess. 4:13–18).

However, shifts of this kind are of a very different order from the proposition that Paul gradually abandoned future apocalyptic as the center of his thought. For in that case a *fundamental* change in Paul's gospel must be posited, that is, the change to a different center of his gospel. The result of such a proposition would be that the interrelation in Paul between the coherent center of the gospel and the contingent circumstances to which it addresses itself would change into something very different, that is, the gospel itself would become simply a contingent variable and lose its coherent and abiding integrity.

(2) Such a radical change in the coherent center of the gospel is indeed advocated by the proponents of realized eschatology. But the shift in Paul from eschatology to ecclesiology would signify a total reversal of his prior convictions. It would mean a complete abandonment of a vision of the world that entails a cosmic redemption and a public vindication of God's promise and purpose that—as we have seen—is undergirded by an imminent expectation that hopes for the dissolution of all dualistic structures in the world.

Moreover, when the doctrine of the church is viewed as the key to Paul's thought, apocalyptic and Christology tend to become so conflated and fused that the "body of Christ" (= the church) becomes identified with the risen body of Christ and the organic growth of the church is substituted for the parousia of Christ. Such a conflation of apocalyptic and Christology results in an inflation of the concept of the church in Paul and has dire consequences for the relation of church and world and their mutual relation to the coming apocalyptic triumph of God.

A mystical doctrine of the church catholic here threatens to displace the idea of the church as the preliminary vanguard of the kingdom of God, and the notion of Christ as the fulfillment of all of God's purposes leads to such a spiritualization of God's promises to his created world that the structures of the world itself remain untouched by them. Moreover, this conception heightens the dualism between church and world and forgets that in Paul church and world are joined together in a bond of solidarity—so that the church cannot boast in a "realized eschatology" for itself over against the world. The communal solidarity of church and world marks the church instead as a community of hope while it groans and labors for the redemption of the world.

The strength of the *existentialist analysis of Paul's gospel* lies in its focus on the distinctiveness of Paul's call and apostolate that forms the exclusive center of his preaching: "I decided to know nothing among you except Jesus Christ and him crucified" (1 Cor. 2:2). Paul's commitment celebrates the folly and stumbling block of the cross of Christ as the power and wisdom of God (1 Cor. 1:18–25). Paul's stumbling block as a Jew had been the resurrection of the *crucified* Messiah that had compelled him to persecute Christian believers. And it was the reversal of that perception that constituted his Christian call and apostolate. This new perception, that a *crucified* Messiah, cursed by the Law, was indeed vindicated by God and installed by him as the Son of God, implied as its necessary consequence the cruciform existence of believers: "I have been crucified with Christ; it is no longer I who live, but Christ who lives in me" (Gal. 2:20). Commitment to the crucified Messiah entails the awareness of the saving presence of God in the believer in a peculiar, even contradictory, manner because it signifies the reversal of all worldly estimates as to what constitutes God's blessing and peace in life. Rudolf Bultmann expresses this view eloquently:

> The resurrection is not a mythological event adduced in order to prove the saving efficacy of the cross, but an article of faith just as much as the meaning of the cross itself. Indeed, faith in the resurrection is really the same thing as faith in the saving efficacy of the cross, faith in the cross as the cross of Christ. Hence, you cannot first believe in Christ and then in the strength of that faith believe in the cross. To believe in Christ means to believe in the

cross as the cross of Christ. The saving efficacy of the cross is
not derived from the fact that it is the cross of Christ; it is the
cross of Christ because it has this saving efficacy. Without that
efficacy, it is the tragic end of a great man.[8]

Bultmann points to the centrality of the cross as the core of
Paul's thought; and the truth of the cross entails the existential
decision of becoming cross-bearers: "to believe in the cross of
Christ is to make the cross of Christ our own, to undergo cruci-
fixion with him."[9] To be sure, not every interpreter of Paul
would agree with Bultmann's existentialist interpretation of the
cross, but he typifies all those interpreters who select the cross
as Paul's distinctive contribution to Christian thought. Indeed,
the strength of this position lies in its emphasis on what has been
called the "exclusive particularity" of Paul's gospel. If the abiding and ultimate signature of God's incursion into our world is
the cross of Christ, and if the abiding message of the gospel
concerns the cross and our participation in it, then no other
center of Paul's gospel seems possible, and every other aspect of
Paul's thought becomes simply an effluence from that center.

Paul's vocabulary of redemption seems to confirm this estimate. The paradox of cross and resurrection persists in the paradox of Christian life: the foolishness of God is the wisdom of
God (1 Cor. 1:23–24); the power of Christ is made perfect in
weakness (2 Cor. 12:9) so that Paul confesses, "for when I am
weak, then I am strong" (2 Cor. 12:10); the treasure of the light
of the gospel of glory is contained in earthen vessels, "so that
the transcendent power belongs to God and not to us" (2 Cor.
4:7). The so-called catalogues of crisis situations can be understood only in terms of this paradoxical strength amidst weakness (2 Cor. 4:7–12; 6:3–10; 11:23–29; also 1 Cor. 4:9–13). Indeed the focus of the apostle's glory is the cross of Christ: "Far
be it from me to glory except in the cross of our Lord Jesus
Christ, by which the world has been crucified to me, and I to the
world" (Gal. 6:14).

If the centrality of the cross could absorb all the other dimensions of Paul's thought, a radical reinterpretation of the apocalyptic traditions that Paul had inherited should be in order. In that case, a christologically oriented apocalyptic could not be maintained as the key to Paul's thought and would instead have to be characterized as a distortion of that thought. We must be aware that the cross-centered proposal can appeal not only to the participatory language of Paul ("to be in Christ," "to be crucified with Christ," and so forth) but also to the central redemptive metaphors of justification, redemption, reconciliation, and adoption. All these metaphors focus on the death and resurrection of Jesus Christ and translate its meaning for Christian believers. Moreover, these metaphors refer in nearly all cases to what *has been* accomplished in Christ; and even when they contain a futurist referent, that referent can be interpreted as the continuing demand of the gospel on its hearer to appropriate the cross and its saving character ever anew. For the word of the gospel makes the cross an abiding reality for the believer rather than something that lies in the historical past and can be taken for granted.

The centrality of the cross also underscores the anthropological focus of Paul's gospel. For there can be no doubt that for Paul the major apocalyptic forces are not the usual apocalyptic angelic inhabitants of the heavenly regions but those ontological powers that determine the human situation, that is, those powers that comprise the "field" of death, sin, the Law, and the flesh. Apocalyptic cosmology has a clear anthropological focus in Paul because his thought concentrates on the human condition and its determinants prior to the coming of faith and under faith.[10] And these power structures have been defeated by the cross of Christ. Therefore they no longer continue their sovereign rule. "Christ is the end of the law" (Rom. 10:4) for believers and the end of the dominion of sin and the flesh in our members (Rom. 6:1–23; Gal. 5:13–25). The primary beneficiary of the cross, then, seems to be us human beings in our present condition and not some speculative cosmic future.

Moreover, it can be argued that even if some elements of Paul's thought permit a future apocalyptic dimension (in letters like 1 Thessalonians, 1 Corinthians, and Romans), such an apocalyptic component does not fit into the core of Paul's thought. This is especially the case when one considers letters like Galatians and 2 Corinthians that are not oriented toward a future apocalyptic and moreover focus on the death of Christ rather than on his resurrection and its future consequences.

Above all, proponents of the exclusivistic theology of the cross in Paul can appeal to the history of Pauline interpretation. From Augustine to Luther, Calvin, Barth, and Bultmann, the signature of Pauline theology has been "the cross alone is our theology" *(crux sola nostra theologia)*.

Notwithstanding the strength of these arguments, I contend that the proponents of such a theology of the cross short-circuit Paul in four ways:

(1) The cross is here construed as an alternative to Paul's future apocalyptic or as the event that absorbs it. In other words, *the larger context in which the cross functions in Paul is overlooked.* This proposal errs not because of its focus on the cross, but because of its inability to locate the cross within the embrace of the future apocalyptic structure of Paul's thought. A focus on the *cross alone* distorts the relation between cross and resurrection.

(2) A view of the cross that draws the resurrection into the cross as the exclusive referent of its meaning interprets the cross and resurrection as completed events, that is, as events which mark the closure of God's redemptive acts. Nonetheless, cross and resurrection must be understood as future-oriented events. Unless we understand that just as the resurrection is inseparably linked to the cross, so the cross is inseparably linked to the resurrection, we distort the significance of both. Because the resurrection of Christ is the "first fruits" of the general resurrection, it is an inaugurating event and not a closure event. The cross of the *risen* Lord participates in this forward dimension of the res-

urrection: it anticipates the time when not only its judgment of the world will be confirmed in the last judgment but also its saving character will be confirmed by the visible love and glory of God.

(3) Just as the cross is not the alternative to Paul's future apocalyptic, so Paul's paradoxical statements about life in the midst of death and about the divine presence in the midst of human suffering must not be viewed as alternatives to Paul's future apocalyptic. The death and resurrection of Christ are related to each other not only in a dialectical but also in a consecutive manner. The dialectics of power *and* weakness, life *in the midst of* death, or our glorying *in* the cross express a vital aspect of Paul's gospel. Yet this *dialectic* becomes a static paradox when it is not viewed in the context of the apocalyptic *sequence* of life after death. The centrality of the cross, then, not only defines the character of the apocalyptic hope but also must be understood in the context of the apocalyptic hope—a hope directed toward the coming of God, when life's burdensome contradictions will be "swallowed up by life" (2 Cor. 5:4).

(4) When the centrality of the cross is divorced from its apocalyptic components, it not only promotes an individualism that disregards the cosmic solidarity of Paul's anthropology but also leads to such an exclusive emphasis on Christology that it collapses future apocalyptic into the Christ-event. Christ is now viewed not as the "first fruits" of the future resurrection of the dead, but as the total "fullness of God" (Col. 1:19), and the Spirit becomes now equated with that manifestation of God's glory that only the future will disclose.

A theology of the cross, then, that is unrelated to the resurrection as the "first fruits" of the kingdom of God and of the future resurrection of the dead encourages not only an individualistic distortion of Paul's gospel but also an exclusivist centering of that gospel on the Christ-event. And so it can chart our future as human beings only in terms of our individual obedience to the cross and of a cruciform life. It has nothing to say about the future of the world or our future communal solidarity in the kingdom of God. The future resurrection of the dead now becomes transposed into a doctrine of a post-mortem afterlife for the individual believer. Moreover, an exclusivistic theology of the cross becomes easily transformed into a passion-mysticism; it silences Paul's apocalyptic hope for that time when God will defeat the power of death in the world and so reveal his opposition to suffering and evil.

Although the opposition between a "theology of glory" and Paul's "theology of the cross" has been a standard canon of interpretation in the history of Protestant thought, such a strict antithesis between them is not tenable for Paul's apocalyptic theology. To be sure, a theology of glory without the cross is unthinkable for Paul. But a doctrinaire theology of the cross contradicts Paul's hope in the "theo-logy" of God's imminent glory, which already casts its rays into our world.

The location of Paul's center in a *salvation-historical* scheme has become prominent since the work of Oscar Cullman.[11] Unlike the options of realized eschatology and of an exclusivistic concentration on the cross, the salvation-historical scheme emphasizes the significance of Paul's future eschatology.

Cullman does full justice to the nature of the interim time between the "already" of Christ and the "not yet" of the future consummation of the kingdom of God. He introduces the analogy of D-Day and V-Day of World War II to illustrate the tension of Christian life:

> The expectation thus continues to exist just as in Judaism. What the Jews expected of the future is still expected of the future; but the future event is no longer the center of redemptive history; rather, that center lies now in a historical event. The center has been reached, but the end is still to come. I may illustrate this idea by an example: *the decisive battle in a war may already have occurred in a relatively early stage of the war, and yet the war still continues* [italics mine]. Although the decisive effect of the battle is perhaps not recognized by all, it nevertheless already means victory. But the war must still be carried on for an undefined time, until "Victory Day."[12]

Cullman thus emphasizes the bifocal character of Paul's thought. The salvation-historical scheme points, however, to the central interpretive problem of Paul's future apocalyptic. What is at stake here is not the often repeated proposition of the tension between the "already" of the Christ-event and the "not yet" of the kingdom of God, but rather their precise *quality* and *weight*. How do we understand the relative weight of the two foci of the ellipse—the Christ-event and the coming parousia? This issue is crucial because it determines the cutting edge of Paul's apocalyptic thought. If we, for instance, posit a *shifting* center to Paul's eschatology—moving the emphasis *from* the parousia *to* the Christ-event—we have severely compromised its apocalyptic character. Cullmann characterizes Christ as the "center" or "midpoint" of Paul's faith and Paul's future eschatology as a variable that was and is inherently open to temporal shifts and changes. When he states, "Eschatology is not put aside, but it is dethroned and this holds true both chronologically and essentially,"[13] he not only neglects the urgency of time in early Christian experience but also allows a Christ-centered salvation-history to displace God's coming triumph. The eclipse of the imminent cosmic expectation of the kingdom of God coincides here with a view that considers the Christ-event essentially as the center and fulfillment of all of God's promises. And so the eschatological consummation becomes an *extrapolation* from the central event of Christ. Cullman ignores Paul's interpretation of the Christ-event as the event that *anticipates* the kingdom of God. The result is that the parousia of Christ functions here like a proper postlude, which is no longer the center of the musical composition. Whenever the fervent longing for the final victory of God becomes secondary to the present reign of Christ, New Testament theo-logy is absorbed into Christology and the future thrust of the gospel evolves into an almost exclusive preoccupation with the present task of the church and its possibilities in an ongoing world.

Cullmann's conception of the relation of eschatology to missions manifests this tendency. Whereas Paul relates eschatology

and the mission of the church dialectically so that neither future
eschatology suffocates the missionary task nor the missionary
task suspends future eschatology, Cullmann understands Paul
along the lines of Mark where the end is made dependent on the
proclamation of the gospel to the whole world: "And the gospel
must first be preached to all nations" (Mark 13:10; cf. Matt.
24:14). We can say, then, that Cullmann interprets the Pauline
tension between the "not yet" and the "already" in terms of the
scheme of Luke-Acts—where, to be sure, the expectation of the
end is not surrendered, but where its priority, if not its intensity,
is suspended. Indeed, the Messiah who is taken up into heaven
"will come in the same way as you saw him go into heaven"
(Acts 1:11), but the worldwide mission "to the end of the earth"
(Acts 1:8) is the prior task of the disciples.

Thus when Paul's theological center is located in a salvation-
historical scheme, that scheme fails to take account of what for
Paul is the cutting edge of his apocalyptic: the fervent, Spirit-
inspired longing for the coming cosmic triumph of God as the
necessary consequence of the death and resurrection of Jesus
Christ.

A NEW CHALLENGE

I suggest then that the center of Paul's thought is to be located
in his christologically determined future apocalyptic. The nonapocalyptic interpreters of Paul discussed above are indeed able
to bridge the gap between the "historical" Paul and the present.
However, interpreters of Paul who propose a realized eschatology, a one-sided theology of the cross, or a salvation-history
solution to bridging the gap all interpret the relation between the
Christ-event and the cosmic future kingdom of God in favor of
an exclusivistic focus on the Christ-event that either absorbs future apocalyptic or reduces its importance.

I have completed my discussion of the major nonapocalyptic
interpreters of Paul's thought. At this point a more difficult task
awaits us, that is, whether an apocalyptic interpretation of Paul
is still a viable option for Christians today. The difficulties of

such a proposal are indeed self-evident: How can people today continue to believe in an imminent expectation of the kingdom of God? Has not the continuation of the historical process itself nullified such an expectation, a process seemingly based on an obsolete world view anyway?

6

Paul's Apocalyptic Gospel: Obsolete or Relevant?

It is my conviction that Paul's apocalyptic gospel presents a challenge to the church. Moreover, if this challenge is faithful to Paul's own thought, then his apocalyptic can neither be eliminated nor reinterpreted in such a way just to accommodate our tastes and sensitivities. If this challenge is to stand it must overcome at least four fundamental objections which have been raised against apocalyptic: the obsolete character of the apocalyptic world view, the misleading "literal" language of apocalyptic for Christian spirituality, the argument that apocalyptic has a purely symbolic significance, and the refutation of future apocalyptic by the ongoing process of history. Objections like these have exercised an immense pressure on the interpretation of Paul's gospel. The result is that—apart from some sectarian aberrations—the mainstream of Christian thought has eliminated, suppressed, or reinterpreted the apocalyptic of Paul and the rest of the New Testament. Most interpreters, as we saw above, opt for a Christ-centered approach to Paul's gospel, one that presumably can absorb the supposedly peripheral apocalyptic forms of his message. And indeed, once future eschatology moved out of the mainstream of church life, it was co-opted by heretical movements that proved to be an embarrassment to the truth of the gospel. A literalist reading of scriptural imagery, combined with speculative predictions, all too often promoted and continues to promote an egomaniacal enthusiasm and apocalyptic paranoia which caused and causes not only a distortion of the gospel but also a delusion of the human soul.

I will proceed as follows: a discussion of the first three objections leads to a debate on the meaning of the resurrection of Christ. It not only discloses the inconsistencies that a nonapocalyptic interpretation of the resurrection entails but also underscores the ethical dimensions of an apocalyptic reading of the resurrection. Subsequently I investigate the adequacy of the interpretation of millenarian movements by the social sciences; and finally I confront the fourth objection, that is, the relation of apocalyptic to the continuation of the historical process.

A THEOLOGICAL PERSPECTIVE
ON APOCALYPTIC

Reflection on the methodological problem must precede a discussion of the first three objections listed above. The problem of theological method is provoked by the contrary claims of theology and the social sciences, that is, anthropology, sociology, and psychology. For how do we negotiate the theological assertion that claims that Paul's apocalyptic gospel is the word of God for the church in terms of the insights of the social sciences? Must we presuppose that the findings of the social sciences constitute the norm in terms of which the theological claim of the gospel must be adjudicated and accommodated? Or does the theological claim of the gospel constitute the norm, so that it is not affected or qualified by theories of the social sciences? And if we admit that the insights of human experience—as described and cataloged by the social sciences—can be neglected only at the cost of the intelligibility of the Christian theological claim, does this admission imply that the Christian theological claim must be adjusted to the normative stature of scientific theory?

It should be clear that this methodological issue cannot be resolved by such alternatives. These simple alternatives should give way to a correlation of perspectives, meaning that both theological and scientific perspectives must be allowed to cooperate in a fruitful way—by a synthesis. Such a correlation of perspectives is necessary because frequently we either fuse the two perspectives or allow them simply to collide. The first possibility occurs when, fearful of a confrontation with the findings of science, we dictate imperially that history and theology are harmoniously related. A second possibility presents itself when historians reject theological claims as subjective and arbitrary or when theologians disdain historical claims as a threat to their dogmatic assertions. A collision of perspectives occurs, for instance, when Paul's apocalyptic is defended only on the basis of a biblicistic rigidity or on the basis of an inspired view of scripture. As I have already indicated, the method of the neo-apocalyptic movement must be rejected on these grounds. But a collision also occurs when the human sciences transgress the proper boundaries of their inquiry and in their rejection of theological claims absolutize their own canons of explanation. This happens, for instance, when psychological or sociological factors are adduced as all-sufficient explanations of millenarian movements. The insight that the process of understanding is basically a unified process in which historical and theological understanding ultimately fuse is what is at stake in a fruitful synthesis of perspectives. In terms of the debate on myth—and for our purpose, especially apocalyptic myth—it becomes clear that this debate has too often neglected the synthesis of historical and theological claims.

Rudolf Bultmann, for instance, adopts a stance toward myth that *contrasts* the scientific world view with the world of myth and so robs the apocalyptic myth of its cosmic-historical intent.[1] Bultmann's objection to myth is twofold: it is not only obsolete language but also misleading language. It is obsolete because it represents a primitive world view that is no longer possible for us moderns to maintain. And it is misleading because it speaks about transcendent reality in this-worldly terms. Although Bultmann rejects the nineteenth-century attempt to "de-myth" Paul's gospel (that is, simply to remove its mythical elements) for the sake of modern intelligibility as arbitrary, his own program of demythologizing (that is, of interpreting the whole of

Paul's gospel in terms of an existentialist interpretation that addresses authentic human existence) takes place in a twilight zone between "de-mything" and an interpretation of the true intention of myth itself. Bultmann claims that insofar as myth is *obsolete* language it needs to be removed; but insofar as it is *misleading* language it must be interpreted according to its own (existentialist) intent. To what extent, however, has Bultmann surrendered the permanent theological claim of Paul's apocalyptic? What compels him to decide that Paul's claim must be radically reinterpreted for modern people? The answer lies for Bultmann in the contrary claims of the scientific world view and the world of apocalyptic myth. That conflict dominates his interpretation, and thus the myth must be interpreted in a way that does not collide with the scientific world view.

Thus, when Bultmann opposes the literal understanding of myth to its anthropological intent, he dismisses the relation of the literal to the real and opts instead for the figurative meaning of the myth. This amounts to an oversimplification of the problem. For the "literal" meaning of the myth has surely a double component. It means not only a literal interpretation of its metaphorical imagery, but also a literal interpretation of *its real intent*—conveyed in and under its use of images. Bultmann now collapses the double component of the term "literal" into one interpretive structure. He correctly insists on a nonliteral interpretation of apocalyptic imagery; but because he also insists on a nonliteral interpretation of the real intent of the myth, he arbitrarily locates the meaning of the myth solely in its anthropological significance. Therefore, he bypasses the realistic intent of the apocalyptic language, that is, its insistence on the reality of the hope in the cosmic victory of God at the end-point of history.

Although the subsequent discussion of myth has moved away from Bultmann's position in according myth a much more positive value, Bultmann's interpretation of myth remains especially significant because he has set the terms for the subsequent debate and has raised the theological issue in an acute manner. The central issue is, indeed, whether the meaning of the apocalyptic myth is exhausted by its anthropological intent. And yet, disagreement about the scope and nature of the anthropological intent of apocalyptic myth cannot negate the theological question whether Paul's apocalyptic world view should be collapsed into its anthropological intent. When Paul Ricoeur, for instance, criticizes Bultmann for not honoring the fullness of the language of myth and its enduring value and states that "myth's literal function must be suspended, but its symbolic function must be affirmed,"[2] he in fact restricts the meaning of myth to its human function of symbolic speech and of expressing ultimate meanings.

In order to get a better grasp of what is at stake theologically in the interpretation of Paul's apocalyptic, we must address the difficult question of the relation of symbolism to the nature of truth. After all, meaning and truth do not simply coincide in life. The meaning of a symbol may constitute an ultimate meaning for its maker, but it is not therefore to be granted the status of truth. The meaning of a myth or a symbol needs verification by a referent outside itself in order to qualify as truth. It makes a crucial difference whether we locate the truth and meaning of a symbolic universe purely in the perception of its creator or whether we locate its truth in a referent that lies outside the creator's own world of meaning—that is, in an ontological truth-claim.

In other words, I wish to assert that the claim for a *literal* understanding of Paul's apocalyptic is directly related to the truth-claim of his gospel. That truth-claim is part and parcel of the confessional stance of the Christian. Therefore the constant suppression by scholars of the literal claim of Paul's apocalyptic is for the Christian not simply a rejection of Paul's so-called primitive world view, but to the contrary the rejection of a central confessional and theological claim. The rejection of the literal claim of Paul's apocalyptic in favor of its interpretation in terms of symbolic language is for Christians unacceptable. It represents for them an inappropriate identification of literal language with obsolete and misleading language and a simplistic identification of figurative language with realistic language. In other words, Paul's apocalyptic is not simply exhausted by its anthropological-symbolic function, as if its meaning is sufficiently explained by the symbolic activity of Paul and his perceptual creativity. In that case the truth of Paul's apocalyptic would lie exclusively in its own field of meaning without the possibility of a referent that transcends Paul's human imagination. It is only such a transcendent referent that gives the apocalyptic myth a meaning—grounded in the truth-claim of the gospel as God's word to us. (And the truth-claim of the apocalyptic gospel of Paul is in turn based on the historicity of the resurrection of Christ that evokes the hope for God's ultimate apocalyptic triumph.)

Paul's apocalyptic is not to be defended on the basis of a biblicistic rigidity. It is impossible to transfer Paul's first-century world directly into our own world. Rather, Paul's apocalyptic is to be *defended* on two grounds: (1) It offers the church today—living in a different world and time from Paul's—the catalytic power to reflect on his language in a new way. (2) Without Paul's apocalyptic the theological truth-claim of his gospel is jeopardized. In other words, if apocalyptic is an integral part of Paul's gospel, then the truth-claim of that gospel as God's word for the church becomes, if not indefensible, at least compromised if apocalyptic is removed from it.

Paul's apocalyptic is not an obsolete and/or peripheral ornamental husk that can be eliminated or reinterpreted in such a way that the *core* of his gospel remains unaffected. As I contend, Paul's apocalyptic is the necessary consequence of the truth of the gospel; he does not celebrate apocalyptic *notwithstanding* Christ but *because of* Christ. For the death and resurrection of Christ are future-oriented events, not "closure" events. Thus the gospel of Christ today becomes severely distorted when we ignore this central issue.

PAUL'S APOCALYPTIC AND THE
RESURRECTION OF CHRIST

The modern debate about the resurrection illustrates this. For Paul and the early Christians, the resurrection of Christ was meaningful not just because it vindicated the death of Christ, but especially because it vindicated the death of Christ as the overture to the final resurrection of the dead, that is, as the anticipation of God's self-vindication *over* his world and *on behalf of* his world. The modern debate now illustrates the embarrassment about the *necessary connection* in Paul between the resurrection of Christ and the future resurrection of the dead. Because it was impossible for many modern theologians to deny the resurrection of Christ and maintain the integrity of Paul's gospel in any sense at all, and because it was equally deemed impossible to maintain an obsolete apocalyptic world view that predicated the sudden and imminent end of world history, the necessary connection between the two resurrections had to be cut apart. When, however, the apocalyptic future resurrection of the dead was rejected, the apocalyptic meaning of the resurrection of Christ also had to be rejected. Instead the resurrection of Christ came to be viewed as a completed event, that is, as the climactic fulfillment of all of God's promises. The result of this procedure was a radical spiritualization of the Christ-event: it came to be viewed exclusively in terms of its meaning for human spirituality.

This spiritualistic interpretation of the Christ-event was considered an easy price to pay for the help it provided in overcoming an embarrassing "primitive" apocalyptic world view. From henceforth the historical process was allowed to run its continuing course without any "apocalyptic" incursion. However, the spiritualistic interpretation of the Christ-event brought with it a severe loss. The meaning of the gospel for the course of history and the future of the world was suppressed, and its meaning was now restricted to the spatial relation of the transient (below) to the eternal (above). In this manner the future hope in the resurrection of the dead at the end of history became transposed into a doctrine of the translation of the individual soul to heaven immediately after death. The history of the world was now viewed as the permanent stage upon which Christian activity takes place, that is, the stage for ethics and missions, whereas the natural and historical world as such was no longer considered to be the object of God's saving and judging intervention. And so Christian hope was no longer directed to the cosmic theophany of the glory of God but became restricted either to hope in a God who "is always One who comes" and is "permanent futurity" (Bultmann),[3] or to hope in the Spirit-endowed ethical activity of Christians in the world (C.H. Dodd and Walter Rauschenbusch).[4] One did not notice that the reduction of Paul's hope in the public manifestation of God's glory actually caused a crippling of the ethical imagination. Ethical activity focused now either on the private sphere of the individual or on the social power of Christian witness in the world. And ethical exhortation concerned itself either with the existential authenticity of the individual or with the social responsibility of the Christian. The demand for a social gospel, however authentic its impulse, nonetheless contained a tragic aspect which was not given due recognition. For it should be clear that unless that demand is viewed against the horizon of *God's initiative* in bringing about his kingdom, it threatens to become a romantic exaggeration of the ethical capability of the Christian. For although Christians must do battle against the power of death and against the unjust power structures of this world, they should not overrate their own capabilities. Otherwise God's will and power become too easily identified with the will and power of Christians and the church so that Christians succumb to the heretical slogan, "On this earth God's work is truly our own." In other words, unless Christians know that their ethical activity is essentially an anticipation of that greater reality of God's coming kingdom, they cannot but wonder about the futility of their efforts in view of the overwhelming structures of evil and suffering in our world. And unless Christians know that it is their task to establish nothing but beachheads of the kingdom of God in this world, then not only the sheer magnitude of the ethical task will suffocate them, but also their frequent inability to measure ethical progress will stifle them.

We can state the issue theologically as follows: if we view the relation between the Christ-event and subsequent Christian life solely as a relation between God's grace that is ours in Christ and the ethical demand of obedience, we distort the meaning of Paul's gospel and its message for us. Christian history after the Christ-event is not simply the working out of God's once-and-for-all action in Christ. It is not merely the demand to conduct ourselves in the light of that once-and-for-all gift of God's grace in Christ. Rather, the ethical demand of Christian life is embraced by two acts of God, that is, by both his past act in Jesus Christ and his future act when the final theophany will usher in the resurrection of the dead and the last judgment. The ethical activity of the Christian then is motivated not only by the power of Christ in the Spirit but also by the beckoning power of God's kingdom. And so both God's *past* act in Christ and his *future* act in the resurrection of the dead converge on Christian life in the present. For only God himself will be able to complete the work that he began in us in Christ (Phil. 1:6).

The resurrection of Christ, then, necessarily points to the future glory of God for its completion. In other words, the resurrection of Christ and the future resurrection of the dead are inseparable. The separation of the resurrection of Christ from the future resurrection of the dead at the parousia not only denies the hope in a future resurrection but also frequently brings with it a denial of the historicity of the resurrection of Christ itself. Because an outright denial of the resurrection of Christ represents a dismantling of Paul's gospel, the resurrection must be accounted for by those who separate the resurrection of Christ from the future resurrection of the dead, albeit in a manner that does not offend modern sensibility. Although for Paul the resurrection of Christ was a historical event that opens up the future of God's coming reign, those interpreters who reject the apocalyptic future are now forced to draw the resurrection of Christ into the same symbolic orbit with which they interpret the apocalyptic future. Indeed, both events stand or fall together. It is not easy to affirm the resurrection as a historical event of God's intervention and power and simply to deny the historical closure or completion-event of the world as due to the same intervention and power. And the inverse holds as well: once you interpret the apocalyptic future in symbolic terms, so also the resurrection of Christ. The price then of not affirming the historical character of the resurrection of Christ is the surrender of the conviction of God's direct eschatological intervention into the historical flow of life.

The "literal" claim of Paul's apocalyptic, then, is not to be assigned to a culturally conditioned language that must be transcended by a more appropriate linguistic medium for our time. I contend that the center of Paul's gospel lies in his apocalyptic interpretation of the Christ-event, so that his apocalyptic is inseparable from the content of the gospel. Thus a faithful rendering of Paul's gospel today cannot separate its apocalyptic *form* from its supposedly abiding nonapocalyptic *content*. Our tendency to make Paul's apocalyptic a time-conditioned variable that does not belong to the core of his gospel must be rejected.

The widespread rejection of the "literal" meaning of Paul's apocalyptic, then, has ominous consequences for the integrity of his gospel because the rejection of Paul's apocalyptic represents a distorted abbreviation of his gospel. The consequences of rejecting the "literal" meaning of his apocalyptic become clear when we consider how frequently this apocalyptic is interpreted in a purely ethical and/or pastoral sense. A purely hortatory or pastoral interpretation of Paul's apocalyptic has become so prevalent among us that it seems as if Paul's proclamation of God's final theophany was only an apt device for exhorting

Christians to action or for consoling them in distress. Such a use of Paul's apocalyptic represents an abuse. Such an interpretation ignores a central Pauline claim: the apocalyptic dawn of God's triumph in Christ provides Paul's gospel with its fundamental ethical motivation.

We must be aware, however, that the relevance of the apocalyptic gospel of Paul for today depends on a careful delineation of its distinctive elements. Otherwise Paul's apocalyptic gospel easily degenerates into the type of apocalyptic represented by Hal Lindsey and others. Paul's apocalyptic only becomes a genuine possibility for us today when his emphasis on the radical transcendence and glory of God over all our reckonings and calculations is given its full weight. Apocalyptic degenerates into speculative knowledge and predictions unless God's end-time is seen within the context of God's radical transcendence *over* history. In this respect the Hebrew Bible's insistence on God's sovereign glory and authority must assist us. For the biblical dialectic of God who is on the one hand the Absolute Sovereign Creator and Redeemer, and on the other hand the one who identifies himself with his people, marks Israel as a people of ardent hope (Isa. 60: 1–22, 61:1–11). But that hope becomes a false hope and a false security when Israel transforms God's promise to her into a scheme of calculation and secret knowledge (Dan. 8:25–27, 9:24–27, 12:6–12). In a similar way Paul—the Christian interpreter of God's ways with Israel—interprets apocalyptic in terms of radical hope, radical surprise, and radical patience (see chapter 3, above). For notwithstanding the signs of the times—whether they point to God's imminent coming or to God's delay—the one necessary and basic sign *has been given* to us in the death and resurrection of Christ. And this one sign determines the character of all future signs. Indeed, it determines the character of Christian hope itself. Just as the event of Jesus Christ was inaugurated by God in an unexpected time and in an unexpected mode, so the completion of that event in the kingdom of God will be equally unexpected because it is in

God's hands alone. Thus to predicate the signs of the times as sure indications of the end of history is to betray the sign of Christ as that of God's own transcendent making.

We may venture the thought that Paul's faith in the radical transcendence of God is not diminished, but heightened, by God's saving intervention in Christ. For, although the vision of the coming kingdom inspires and motivates Paul's apostolic career, that vision translates itself into a radical concern for the "penultimate" rather than into a preoccupation with the "ultimate," that is, a concern for "what is at hand" rather than for "what will be." For that reason Paul consciously subdues apocalyptic imagery and speculation. God's incursion into our history in the death and resurrection of Christ compels Paul to labor for the Lordship of Christ in this world and to do so in the mode of his Lord, that is, in a cruciform way of life. Therefore, he is occupied by "what is at hand" and leaves the hour of God's kingdom in God's hands alone. The transcendence of God, then, is not undone by God's immanence in history in Christ. The One who *has* come to us in Christ *will* come again to complete his redemptive purpose according to his promise. And trust in his faithfulness ceases to be trust when it turns to chronological speculation.

MODERN INTERPRETATIONS OF APOCALYPTIC MOVEMENTS

The truth-claim of Paul's apocalyptic gospel should be tested and enlarged by an inquiry into the findings of the social sciences, that is, those of anthropology, sociology, and the phenomenology of religion. This inquiry is necessary because of my earlier contention (see page 80, above) that a synthesis of historical and theological claims helps us to clarify the issue of apocalyptic and can prevent us from making arbitrary and unintelligible assertions. A dialogue with the social sciences gives us an insight into those aspects of the human condition that evoke apocalyptic aspirations. And unless we adhere to a narrow biblicism that guarantees in advance the literal truth and uniqueness of biblical apocalyptic, we must investigate the phenomenon of apocalyptic in human culture generally in order to understand more adequately the specific quality of the truth-claim of Paul's apocalyptic gospel.

It should be stated at the outset that the social sciences—notwithstanding their various methods, selective emphases, and explanatory devices—agree on at least one point. Their explanations of millenarian movements oppose a theological norm or perspective as in any way decisive for the rise of these movements. To be sure, the theological convictions and aspirations of millenarian movements have been recorded; but they are basically viewed as *reactions to* or *effects of* causes that can be fully understood by nontheological explanations.

Mircea Eliade, for instance, views the steady rise and demise of millenarian movements as a participation of the human spirit in "the myth of the eternal return." This myth considers time important only inasmuch as it participates in the timeless event of mythical time at the beginning, *in illo tempore.** But how then do messianic and millenarian movements which project an end to time share in the archaic ontology of the suppression of time? Eliade explains:

> Messianism hardly succeeds in accomplishing the eschatological valorization of time: the future will regenerate time, that is, will restore its original purity and integrity. Thus, *in illo tempore* is situated not only at the beginning of time but also at its end. . . .
> However, the acceptance and consecration of history by the

---

*In discussing the importance of lunar myths for the archaic conception of the regeneration of time, Eliade remarks: "We may note that what predominates in all these cosmic-mythological lunar concepts is the cyclical recurrence of what has been before, in a word, eternal return. . . . This eternal return reveals an ontology uncontaminated by time and becoming. Just as the Greeks, in their myth of eternal return, sought to satisfy their metaphysical thirst for the 'ontic' and the static, even so the primitive, by conferring a cyclic direction upon time, annuls its irreversibility. Everything begins over again at its commencement every instant. The past is but a prefiguration of the future. No event is irreversible and no transformation is final." Mircea Eliade, *The Myth of the Eternal Return,* trans. Willard R. Trask (Princeton: Princeton University Press, 1971), pp. 88–89.

Judaic ethics does not mean that the traditional attitude is transcended. Messianic beliefs in a final regeneration of the world
themselves also indicate an antihistoric attitude. The irreversibility of historical events and of time is compensated by the limitation of history to time. In the spiritual horizon of Messianism,
resistance to history appears as still more determined than in the
traditional horizon of archetypes and repetitions; if, here, history was refused, ignored or abolished by the periodic repetition
of the Creation and by the periodic regeneration of time, in the
Messianic conception history must be tolerated because it has an
eschatological function, but it can be tolerated only because it is
known that, one day or another, it will cease. . . .

The will to put a final and definitive end to history is itself
still an antihistorical attitude, exactly as are the other traditional
conceptions.[5]

Thus Eliade traces these messianic movements to an archaic
ontology that locates the plenitude of being in a metahistorical
realm and that expresses itself in a variety of mythical stories.

Not only have historians of religion like Mircea Eliade com-
mented on millenarian movements. Social scientists, anthro-
pologists, and historians of culture have made equally important contributions to the subject. According to them, the regular
occurrence of such movements in history is caused by a recurring
set of historical conditions; and these conditions—whether economic deprivation, social dislocation, cultural frustration, or
political oppression—become the occasion for a series of explanations. Millenarianism is therefore often characterized as
the religion of deprived groups—a "religion of the oppressed."[6]
It is set in motion by an experience of radical despair or radical
frustration that propels people to long for total redemption.
And yet the deprivation is not necessarily economic. Often a
sense of cultural deprivation, of social isolation, of political dis-
enfranchisement, or a sense of frustration in the need to confront new situations and a new life style will cause the rise of
these movements.

Various explanations for the conditions motivating these

movements have been suggested, ranging from Marxist theories of economic deprivation and Freudian notions of psychosocial pathology to theories about the participation of humankind in an archaic ontology.* Millenarian movements, then, are frequently understood either as a form of collective paranoia—manifestations of mental illness—or, in more sociological terms, as attempts to create a new social order.[7] Thus many sociologists point to the revolutionary nature of the movements, which reflect a strong awareness of the contradictions between what is and what should be. Millenarianism is here viewed as a movement born out of great distress—distress that is heightened by political helplessness.

Social scientists have uncovered a characteristic of millenarian movements that helps to explain their vitality even in the face of their failure to deliver the promised bliss. The phenomenon of disappointed hope and unfulfilled prophecy usually leads not to the immediate disintegration of the movement, but rather to its revitalization and to vigorous proselytizing activity. The so-called theory of "cognitive dissonance" states that "under certain conditions a religious community whose fundamental beliefs are disconfirmed by events in the world will not necessarily collapse and disband."[8] Instead, the condition of distress and doubt caused by the disconfirmation will stimulate missionary activity. Such missionary activity is based on the assumption that "if more and more people can be persuaded that the system of belief is correct, then clearly it must, after all, be correct."[9]

It is clear that the methodology of the social sciences gives us valuable insights into the way early Christians perceived and structured their social world. Christian apocalyptic, however

---

*Norman Cohn's study of the history of millenarianism in medieval and Reformation Europe (*The Pursuit of the Millennium* [rev. ed., New York: Oxford University Press, 1907]) centers on a psychological explanation. He regards "millenarianism as primarily an outlet for extreme anxiety and as a delusion of despair and treats it as a collective paranoid fantasy born out of irrational fears and fantastic expectations." Yonina Talmon, "Pursuit of the Millennium: The Relation between Religious and Social Change," *Reader in Comparative Religion: An Anthropological Approach,* eds. W. Less and E. Vogt, 2d ed. (New York: Harper & Row, 1965), p. 532.

distinctive in some of its features, seems to originate in a set of circumstances that are quite similar to those that generally produce millenarian movements. Early Christians ascribe their movement to a charismatic-prophetic founder who appeals to a specific class of Jewish society and proclaims the imminence of a new order. This new coming order of the kingdom of God is radically opposed to the values of the present social and religious world. Moreover, the death and resurrection of the founder of the movement established a cohesive community of the disaffected that knows itself to be already representing God's new coming order in this world and thus rejects the representatives of the contemporary power structures. The apocalyptic world view and life style of the early Christian community therefore shares basic features with all similar movements in history. And it seems quite true that "the uneven relation between expectations and the means of their satisfaction"[10]—a prominent theory among social scientists for explaining the millenarian movements—provides an important explanation for our understanding of the apocalyptic phenomenon.

From a theological point of view, however, the question must be seriously raised to what extent this method is capable of providing a sufficient explanation for Paul's apocalyptic. This question arises because of three considerations.

(1) When the sociological method claims more than a partial explanatory power for its empirical findings, and when it imperially denies a theological explanation, it absolutizes itself and transcends its own competence.

(2) A theological estimate of Paul's apocalyptic cannot be satisfied with an explanatory theory of "situational incongruity."[11] Rather it insists on a delineation of the specific *quality* and *motivation* of that incongruity. Whatever else may be true about economic, political, and social deprivations or frustrations of the Pauline communities, their apocalyptic stirrings transcend these factors because they are caused by a faith that

by necessity expressed itself in an apocalpytic of a distinct type*
—deriving from a particular set of convictions that are unintelligible apart from the history of Israel's faith and its modified interpretation by Paul after the Christ-event. Paul's apocalyptic, then, cannot be adequately understood if we fail to grasp its determination by the particularity of Israel's faith.

(3) The specificity of Paul's apocalyptic is ultimately unintelligible for the Christian unless the revelatory claim of that apocalyptic is understood. For that revelatory claim is—as we have argued—*inseparable* from the claim of Paul's gospel as God's word. To reject this claim as dogmatic or arbitrary is only then appropriate when it fails the test of intelligibility. However, if the process of understanding Paul's apocalyptic legitimately involves its revelatory claim, then a theological explanation of Paul's apocalyptic has a rightful place in the process of understanding. Nonetheless, the introduction of a theological evaluation of Paul's apocalyptic should not suggest a defense of all forms of apocalyptic. From the Pauline perspective, many apocalyptic movements may have to be characterized as pathological, in the psychological or sociological sense. It is my contention that Paul's apocalyptic not only has a distinctiveness that differentiates it from other forms of apocalyptic but also has a revelatory claim on those who confess the redemptive character of God's act in Christ.

---

*Talmon's remarks are pertinent here. Speaking about the application of neo-Marxian theory to millenarian movements, she says, "These studies also make manifest some of its inherent limitations. By and large, religion is treated here as an ideology which just *expresses* concrete socio-economic interests rather than *moulds* and *directs* them. It is primarily an instrument in the political struggle. Its 'pie in the sky' or mystical versions act as opiate to the people and help to preserve the status quo. Its this-worldly, activist and future-oriented versions act as expressions of the drive towards change. On the theoretical level, religion is denied any independent causal significance and there is no adequate analysis of internal, partly independent processes in the religious sphere." Talmon, "Pursuit of the Millennium: The Relation between Religious and Social Change," *Reader in Comparative Religion: An Anthropological Approach,* eds. W. Lessa and E. Vogt, 2d ed. (New York: Harper & Row, 1965), p. 536; italics mine.

PAUL'S APOCALYPTIC AND THE DELAY
OF THE PAROUSIA

For Christians today, the strongest argument for rejecting a future apocalyptic is undoubtedly the ongoing process of history itself. What else does the continuity of the historical process mean but the decisive *breakdown for us* of Paul's hope in the impending apocalyptic end of history? And what else remains but to translate his gospel in such a manner that the unconditional love of God in Christ as the abiding core of the gospel is not obscured by the imposition of an obsolete and untenable world view? All this is even more true if in fact the imminent confirmation of the hope is a basic element of Paul's apocalyptic that cannot be arbitrarily located on an extended time line that disappears forever—into the future.

Are not we then compelled to devise rationalizations to compensate for the delay of the parousia by surrendering the hope in its imminent arrival? In fact, such rationalizations have constituted the strategies of millenarian movements and the Christian church alike. Talmon remarks:

> These movements are sometimes able to develop a body of exegesis which accounts for the delay and keeps the hope alive. A frequent solution is the switch from a short-range radical millenarism to a long-range and more or less attenuated version of it. Another solution is refraining from fixing any definite date, but still keeping the hope of the speedy delivery in full force. Wilson's study of the Christadelphians proves that such a solution is feasible and can work for a considerable length of time without serious modification of the original doctrine.[12]

Martin Werner has argued in a similar vein that the delay of the parousia was the single most important factor in shaping the development of Christian doctrine.[13] Indeed, it cannot be denied that the history of Christian doctrine has been shaped to a considerable extent by reinterpreting or undoing the eschatology of the early church. And even within the canon of the New Testament, some authors are aware of the delay of the parousia and attempt to come to terms with it. An atmosphere may have prevailed in postapostolic times in which the Jewish apocalyptic world view, with its passion for the public manifestation of God's final righteousness and victory, ceased to be the focal concern. In such a situation the apocalyptic framework is discarded and transposed into something else. And so the tension inherent in the interaction of the twin foci of the Christ-event and the final glory of God snaps and collapses.

The prevailing option in the history of Christian thought has been the fusion of the "not yet" of the future glory with the "already" of the Christ-event so that the passion for the imminent arrival of the kingdom of God was neutralized. Future apocalyptic tended to become instead a "doctrine about the last things" or a philosophical statement about a far-removed conclusion to the cosmos so that the end-time corresponds to primeval time, and the end of the creation to its beginning. It seems that the more the church defined itself apart from its Jewish heritage, the less apocalyptic it became. But, as we have noticed, even within the New Testament canon a shift takes place from a radical hope in the end of history to a qualified hope or even to a suspension of that hope. Documents such as 2 Peter, 2 Thessalonians, and Luke-Acts adopt a solution that *postpones* the final apocalyptic hour, whereas Ephesians, Colossians, and the Johannine corpus *spiritualize* it by conflating the two foci of the Christ-event and the future apocalyptic hour. Even the most specifically apocalyptic sections of the New Testament commence a process which eventually—in the history of the church —leads to a virtual abandonment of faith in the future apocalyptic hour. The device of an apocalyptic *program* often becomes the means to suspend anxiety about the delay of the parousia. For instance, 2 Thessalonians 2 and the synoptic apocalypses (Mark 13; Luke 17 and 21; Matthew 24) all operate with a scheme that posits the occurrence of prior necessary events as the precondition for the parousia.

Let no one deceive you in any way; for that day will not come,
unless the rebellion comes *first*. . . . And *then* the lawless one
will be revealed, and the Lord Jesus will slay him with the breath
of his mouth and destroy him by his appearing and his coming
(2 Thess. 2:3, 8) [italics mine].

And when you hear of wars and rumors of wars, do not be
alarmed; this must take place, but the end is *not yet*. . . . This is
but *the beginning* of the birth-pangs (Mark 13:7, 8) [italics mine].

It seems at first glance that the most apocalyptic book of the New
Testament, Revelation, conforms to that scheme. It has in fact
provided apocalyptic sectarians throughout Christian history
with a detailed sequence of events leading up to the end of history. And the neo-apocalyptic movement of our time would be
inconceivable without Revelation: how else can Hal Lindsey
pinpoint the time of Armageddon and the rapture? By contrast,
however, Revelation with its repetitive series of consecutive
woes is not so programmatic in its intent as is usually supposed.
It does not intend to preach a program of events that pinpoints
our location on the final track of world history; rather, it
preaches the imminence of the parousia to the churches of Asia
Minor. The sequence of its series of woes is not a historical
chronicle, but a dramatic device that stimulates Christian hope
in the impending hour of God's kingdom. Thus the theological
aims of Paul and of Revelation are quite similar, however different the compositional technique of Revelation is from Paul.
Both emphasize the imminence of the apocalyptic hour and
both stress the apocalyptic situation of the present, one that demands a decision about the either/or of allegiance to Christ or
to Satan. However Paul, in contrast to the author of Revelation,
writes letters and not an apocalypse. Therefore, he is able to
subdue apocalyptic imagery in order that the existential power
of apocalyptic not be transmuted into speculation.

The problem of the delay of the parousia then is indeed a
serious one; my solution to this problem will be presented in
chapter 7 below.

PAUL'S APOCALYPTIC IN
MODERN THEOLOGY

Finally, we need to consider how modern theologians have responded to the challenge of Paul's apocalyptic for our time. My brief review will limit itself to the question of how the *necessary* correlation in Paul between the Christ-event and the end-time is interpreted by modern theologians. This correlation is not only one of the central motifs in Paul's apocalyptic but also its most embarrassing aspect for theology today in view of the obvious delay of the parousia.

This issue involves the relation between *anticipation* and *actualization* (or *fulfillment*), and this relationship is crucial for our appropriation of Paul's apocalyptic. For, when the necessity of an apocalyptic actualization is admitted but is accompanied by a denial of its impending factual occurrence, the very structure of Paul's apocalyptic is changed and the relevance of his gospel jeopardized. Macquarrie states the issue well:

> When the end is removed to the distant future, it is taken out of existential time and relegated to calendar time, it shares in the negativity of the "not yet" and it becomes *neutralized* and *ineffective*. It might even induce complacency if it becomes the belief that all things are moving inevitably towards some *far-off divine event,* but the whole business is conceived on such a vast cosmic scale that people feel it has very little to do with them.[14]

Upon reading modern theologians, it is astonishing how inadequately and vaguely this vexing question is addressed. The enormous appeal of neo-apocalypticism—however distorted it may be—comes as no surprise in the face of the evasion of this issue by modern theologians. Their view of the relation between anticipation and actualization is decisively influenced by the natural sciences. The natural sciences have promulgated a widespread notion that has become axiomatic for our dominant culture: that the question of the end of the world by divine intervention is naive and obsolete, or at best a primitive myth of some moral value. Plato's conviction about an enduring world that has a beginning but no end or that of Aristotle that posits neither a beginning nor an end for the world has, as it were, become normative for modern theological interpretations of New Testament apocalyptic.

And so modern theologians present us essentially with three options. The first group denies that the historical correlation of the Christ-event and the imminent end is an issue for Paul and thus has no need to reinterpret Paul's eschatology in a radical manner for the present. The second group admits to the historical correlation of the Christ-event and the imminent end in Paul but reinterprets this structure radically for our time in the face of the delay of the parousia and Paul's obsolete world view. The third group likewise admits to the historical correlation and stresses (in contrast to the second group) the theological necessity of this correlation for our time but denies the relevance or possibility of its chronological actualization.

The first of these three proposals represent primarily the Johannine option of the New Testament, that is, a structure of realized eschatology, viewed as either completed or as in constant process. C.H. Dodd and his followers belong to this group. They view Paul as moving from an emphasis on eschatology to Christ-mysticism and ecclesiology—his major accomplishment. According to Dodd, the Gospel of John has completed this process: "In the Fourth Gospel the crudely eschatological elements in the kerygma are quite refined away . . . sublimated into a distinctive kind of mysticism." [15]

The second group is represented by a wide spectrum of theologians. It ranges from existentialist interpreters such as Rudolf Bultmann[16] and symbolic interpreters such as Amos N. Wilder[17] and Norman Perrin[18] to the process theologians Schubert M. Ogden,[19] Daniel D. Williams,[20] and William A. Beardslee.[21] All are engaged in a radical reinterpretation of the future apocalyptic gospel of Paul (and of the New Testament). John Macquarrie is a typical representative:

Eternal life is the development to the limit of that natural tendency of the human existent to take time and have time rather than just to be in time, and this happens as he extends himself into his past and future, and relates them to his present.[22]

The move to transpose apocalyptic into a radical ethic is prevalent in this group. The imminent triumph of God in Christ is here translated into our human responsibility in Christ for the well-being of the created order. Albert Schweitzer's transposition of apocalyptic into "reverence for life" seems to be the primary model. Robert Jewett, for instance, interprets the apocalyptic mandate to "watch" (Mark 13:33–37) as follows:

To watch is to be prepared for the unexpected. It is to give up the illusions of straight-line extrapolations, the silly assumption that current trends will continue. . . . The proper eschatology is watchful expectancy for the Abba's work and will, and a wary guardedness about the rebounding perversity of humankind. . . . One reason God reserves [the future] in silence is that we are thereby enabled to greet it freshly, to taste his grace in the new dawn of every day. . . . Genuine living is response to the unexpected. The Abba always surprises us, and to live as his children means sitting expectantly on the edge of our seats, waiting to see what happens next.

God is the Abba who loves each of his wayward children unconditionally. . . . The message of the inverted kingdom is that the dynamic love of the Father equalizes all of his children.[23]

In a similar fashion Richard Hiers interprets Jesus' imminent apocalyptic—after declaring it to be an impossible option for us:

If the fulfillment of life is believed to be in the world, a transformed world, Christian faith and life in the meantime might well include the appreciation, enjoyment and affirmation of the creation, through sharing its blessings with others now, and preserving and enhancing these blessings for the generations that come after us.[24]

However noble these sentiments are, they distort the meaning of Paul's and Jesus' apocalyptic because they reinterpret the intent of apocalyptic into its opposite. These interpreters fail to discern that the apocalyptic emphasis on the triumph of God celebrates not only God's initiative in Christ but also God's coming victory in Christ that will be a victory over those powers of evil and death that human initiative and responsibility alone cannot conquer.

Whereas the first group of theologians adheres to a Johannine structure of realized eschatology and the second group to a radical interpretation of the synoptic and Pauline scheme of imminent expectation, the third group adheres to a variation on the theme of 2 Peter. This group responds to the delay of the parousia by *stretching* the time line between the Christ-event and an eventual future kingdom.

Notwithstanding their emphasis on the necessary theological relation of the Christ-event to the end-time, the theologians of this third group fail to recognize that for Paul the end constitutes an actual point of God's intervention in time. Because they bypass this issue, the event of the kingdom of God recedes in their interpretation into the fog of the future—forever. And so the "end-time" expectation of the New Testament has been transposed into a "timeless" expectation. [25]

Wolfhart Pannenberg, for instance, emphasizes the "near" expectation of Jesus and correctly interprets its transition to the "end-time" expectation of the early church after the death and resurrection of Christ. [26] However, he does not interpret this new "end-time" expectation as an intensification of the "near" expectation in a new phase, but rather as the theological justification of a continuing historical process. Such an interpretation of apocalyptic easily transposes futurity into a statement about God's transcendence over history and into a continuing valorization of hope for human life.

And, although Jürgen Moltmann demonstrates the importance of the "coming of God" for our preaching and concentrates on the promises of God in the Bible,[27] he, like Pannenberg, does not address himself to the question of the *urgency* of the hope directed to the coming of God's kingdom at a specific time-point in history. In fact, whether intentionally or not, these theologians of hope construe the end-time more as an event in the realm of ideas than as an actual event. The kingdom of God constitutes for them the final goal and meaning of history. But, because they are convinced that a literal end or completion of history cannot be contemplated, they threatened to accomplish the very opposite of their intent, that is, a philosophy of history that bypasses Paul's expectation of the imminent end of history.

Karl Barth deserves special mention here, although he clearly belongs to this third group as far as future eschatology is concerned. The shift in his position from the "eternal future" of his "Resurrection of the Dead" (1926) and his commentary on Romans[28] to his new posture in *Church Dogmatics* II/1 shows clearly the crucial importance of eschatology for Christian theology. Whereas in his earlier works the qualitative distance between time and eternity preoccupied him so much that it left no room for future eschatology, Barth now struggles in his dogmatics with a new conception of the relation of eternity and time. However, he maintains a fundamental distinction between time and eternity. God is not only "post-temporal" and "pre-temporal" but also "supra-temporal."[29] God's eternity embraces and accompanies all time so that only *for us* future eschatological time is meaningful. Moreover, because God's future kingdom is a mode of his eternity, the historical tension between present and future is, as it were, neutralized. For how new—for God also—can the actualization of the future kingdom be when eternity after time is identical in God with eternity before time? The doctrines of creation and eschatology then seem to be collapsed into God's eternity. The triumph of God in his kingdom is no longer a new event, because the end will only reveal what was actual in God before time. It seems then that the Platonic conception of a timeless eternity still determines

Barth's qualitative distinction of time and eternity. And thus the burning question of the temporal actualization of the kingdom is here muted by other considerations.

This rapid survey of recent theological interpretations of the correlation between the Christ-event and the impending end of history demonstrates the awkward ways in which theologians have dealt with this central aspect of Paul's apocalyptic. And, as John Macquarrie points out, this awkwardness also involves a great theological loss:

> Although this imagery is so remote from our modern ways of thinking, I believe that we can still have an idea of the extraordinary power which such eschatological convictions must have exercised in the lives of the people who held them. To believe that one was living in the face of an end that might happen tomorrow, and, in any case, very soon, must have imparted a tremendous sense of *urgency, responsibility and vitality*. "The appointed time has grown very short." Surely a partial explanation of the amazing energy of the early Christian community is to be sought in its intense conviction of the approaching end. But the conviction of the early community turned out to be mistaken. . . . The end was postponed to the indefinite future. But we must notice that as soon as this happens, eschatology loses most of its power.[30]

In the final chapter I will argue that indeed "eschatology loses most of its power" if the issue of the correlation of anticipation and actualization is not addressed honestly. Our hope in the coming glory of God can be realistically maintained only if it is directly nurtured by its hoped-for actualization in our world.

7

The Challenge
of Paul's Apocalyptic

In order to avoid misunderstanding from the outset, the reader should be aware that the challenge of Paul for today will not be argued on biblicistic grounds. *A direct transfer of Paul's formulation of the gospel to our situation cannot succeed.* Although the coherent and abiding structure of Paul's apocalyptic gospel presents the church today with a challenge that we cannot afford to neglect, this challenge must necessarily bridge the distance between Paul's time and ours. In other words, Paul's apocalyptic gospel has a *catalytic* function for our time. The claim and power of the Pauline text over our present situation must be taken seriously so that the horizon of the text, which so often threatens to become a frozen text, a text buried in the past, is kept open. However, the catalytic function of a text is *not* synonymous with its biblicistic transfer. A biblicistic transfer simply transposes the authority of the Pauline text into our situation and imposes that authority on us, whereas the catalytic function of a text distinguishes between a variety of its elements. It distinguishes between the abiding or coherent elements of the gospel and its time-conditioned or contingent interpretations. Such a distinction allows us to differentiate between the abiding core of Paul's gospel and its various applications. Moreover, it permits us to hear Paul's gospel without giving every word of it a dogmatic, binding authority. If, for example, Paul in his contingent situation does not draw those implications from his apocalyptic gospel that its coherent structure seems to warrant, we cannot simply repeat for ourselves the exegetical moves of Paul.

The catalytic function of Paul's text, then, suggests that the abiding center of the gospel is to be differentiated from the contingent and time-conditioned interpretations of the gospel. If this seems to be an arbitrary method, let me say that the rejection of a biblicistic procedure does not signal the introduction of arbitrary interpretations as if the authenticity of a text can be sacrificed on the altar of relevance. The risk of all interpretation is that it must transcend transliteration if it intends to allow the old words to come to speech again for a new time and a new generation. And the truthfulness of all interpretation is its ability to be faithful to the old text in a new situation.

In what sense, then, can there be a challenge of Paul's apocalyptic for Christians today—when we face not only its failure in the mainstream of Christian doctrine and its inherent theological and existential difficulties but also its denial by the historical process itself? I issue such a challenge by making the following proposals.

APOCALYPTIC: AN ESSENTIAL ELEMENT OF PAUL'S GOSPEL

As we have seen, apocalyptic is an inalienable part of Paul's gospel. The substance of the gospel is for him unthinkable apart from its future apocalyptic mooring. Therefore, apocalyptic thought patterns are not simply an incidental "husk" that can be disregarded or transposed into a nonapocalyptic pattern of thought. And so the truth of Paul's gospel is severely distorted when we remove from it its apocalyptic components.

We cannot pretend to be faithful interpreters of the Pauline gospel if we neglect this insight. The consequence of surrendering Paul's apocalyptic interpretation of the gospel is critical because it affects the very substance of the gospel of Jesus Christ. The retention of Paul's apocalyptic, then, is not for the sake of antiquarian considerations—as if the essence of Paul's thought could be presented without his apocalyptic—but for the sake of the substance of the gospel itself for our time.

Moreover, the post-Pauline history of the church makes it abundantly clear that the gospel itself was jeopardized when nonapocalyptic thought forms displaced its apocalyptic framework. G.W.H. Lampe writes about patristic eschatology:

> Even the orthodox thinkers find it difficult to resist the tendency to allow the eschatological expectation of the primitive Church to give way before one or the other of two points of view, each in its own way incompatible with that expectation.[1]

He elaborates on these two points of view as follows: On the one hand, eschatology is replaced by mysticism, that is, by the thought that through the indwelling of the Spirit the soul becomes spiritual and eventually progresses into the angelic order. On the other hand, eschatology is replaced by a moralism that transforms the hope of the kingdom into a hope of "heaven," the place or state of life in which those who have done good will be rewarded and which is to be won as a price for endurance.

Furthermore, the concept of time implied in the eschatological outlook of the Bible proved to be a decisive obstacle.

> It was inevitable that Gentile Christians should think in terms, not of a "linear" time-sequence, nor of the distinction of "this age" and "the age to come," but rather of a "vertical" relationship between time and eternity, and of the distinction between the temporal and the eternal, the physical and the spiritual, the earthly and the heavenly, the true and the apparent, the reality and the shadow.[2]

The shift from apocalyptic to other forms of thought does indeed constitute something like a "fall of Christendom." Adolf von Harnack's thesis about "the fall of Christendom," which he equated with "the Hellenization of Christianity" and which he attributed to the adoption of the church of Gnostic metaphysical thought, needs to be corrected in several ways.[3] Among those corrections, I want to mention a major one: the fall was not—as Harnack thought—from an interpretation of Jesus as a liberal-rational prophet to the theology of the patristic church, which according to him was dominated by a Gnostic metaphysic. Rather it was a fall from the apocalyptic world of early Christianity to Platonic categories of thought. In other words, the *surrender* of Paul's apocalyptic had indeed a tremendous impact on the history of Christian thought:

(a) The surrender of apocalyptic thought forms produced an alienation of Christianity from its original Jewish matrix, with the result that the messianic expectations of Judaism—evoked by God's promises to Israel—were diverted into a nonapocalyptic Christology.

(b) It produced a spiritualistic interpretation of the gospel. The message of the gospel came to focus almost exclusively on the topic of God and the individual soul—at least in the West—so that it had no relevant word to say about the relation of the gospel to nature and to the structures of this world.

(c) Once the Christ-event became defined in such a way that Christ was conceived as the total "fullness of God" (Col. 1:19) rather than as the "first fruits" of the kingdom of God, the fulfillment of God's promises to Israel was now considered to have been actualized in the Messiah, Jesus Christ. This in turn led to the spiritualization of the promises, and their future reference to the new heaven and new earth of God's cosmic triumph was largely ignored.

(d) Moreover, the surrender of apocalyptic thought forms tended to transfer attention *from* eschatology *to* protology—from a focus on "in the *end* God" to a focus on "in the *beginning* God." This transfer became abundantly clear in the trinitarian and christological controversies of the patristic period. The theory of the immanent Trinity, for instance, left almost no room for a theocentric emphasis on the future of God's coming reign.

(e) The neglect of Paul's cosmic anthropology, which stressed the interrelationship of the creature and the created order, resulted in an increasingly dualistic anthropology. The dualism between spirit and body promoted not only an asceticism that denied human wholeness but also a devaluation of the created order as a vale of tears and as a testing ground for heaven.

(f) In accord with this anthropological pattern, Christian thought identified redemption either with individual bliss or with a conception of the church as the dispenser of the sacraments. Moreover, the apocalyptic conception of the resurrection of the dead, which emphasizes the communal character of all God's people and which refers to the vindication of the creation in the glory of God, was now displaced by the idea of the immortal heavenly status of the individual after death.

(g) The surrender of apocalyptic thought forms promoted an ethic which derived its motivation almost exclusively from God's past saving act in Christ. This meant that the compelling and beckoning power of God's final theophany for ethics was neglected, with the result that Christian ethics often became an ethics of excess, superabundance, and condescension rather than an ethics of cooperative solidarity with human need everywhere. An ethics of excess gravitates easily into a conception of the neighbor as the target of our goodness, love, and compassion. And so we tend to forget that in the light of God's coming glory and vindication all the creatures of God's world are our neighbors because we share with them not only the suffering of the power of death in this world but also the hope in our communal salvation. A responsible apocalyptic recognizes that, without the salvation of our "neighbor" in the world, our final salvation can be neither asserted nor desired. Therefore, without hope for the salvation of all God's creatures, our salvation in Christ remains a temporary and preliminary abode, fraught with the sighing of both the Christian and the creation for the liberating reality of God's kingdom. We who as Christians wander like "the wandering Jew" cannot and should not desire a permanent home in the present structures of this world.

APOCALYPTIC AND ETHICS

Apocalyptic hope, then, *compels ethical seriousness,* because it is existentially impossible to believe in God's coming triumph and to claim his Holy Spirit without a life style that conforms to that faith. And so we must "sit loose" to the striving to find our security in the world and must heed Paul's word:

> I mean, brethren, the appointed time has grown very short; from now on, let those who have wives live as though they had none, . . . and those who buy as though they had no goods, and those who deal with the world as though they had no dealings with it (1 Cor. 7:29–31).

Moreover, apocalyptic hope also compels ethical seriousness because the apocalyptic hour will demand from us a final accountability of our stewardship over God's creation and of our active participation in establishing signs and beachheads of the kingdom in our world.

> For we must all appear before the judgment seat of Christ, so that each one may receive good or evil, according to what he has done in the body (2 Cor. 5:10).

We often fail to realize that the Christian hope in the coming glory of God encompasses the whole created order. This means concretely that our neighbors in the world are persons who not only need us but whom we need as well. And we need them in several ways: First, they clarify the meaning of our life for us and compel us to break out of our various Christian ghettos. Second, they remind us that God's triumph will not take place without the participation of our "neighbors" in it, and so our "neighbors" compel us to struggle together with them for the liberation of all of God's world. Third, and above all, once a person in the world is transformed into "my neighbor," we practice the manner of Paul's apocalyptic gospel, that is, we travel the way of the cross as the way in which God intends to bring about his kingdom.

I dwell on this topic because of the frequent misunderstanding about the inseparable relation of apocalyptic and ethics. Is
not apocalyptic with its exclusive focus on the parousia an invitation to ethical passivity and quietism? Is it not thereby an appeal to ethical irresponsibility or a summons to replace ethical
action with a fatalistic attitude of "leaving it all to God"? And
has not the history of apocalyptic confirmed this—with its sense
of elitism, cosmic favoritism, and withdrawal from that world
into which God sent his Son to bring about its transformation?
I have argued that this is a major misreading of the apocalyptic
motifs of Paul's gospel. To be sure, it must be admitted that
Paul himself in his situation did not always develop and clarify
the practical consequences of his own theological insights, as for
instance in his stance toward the state or in his assessment of the
cultural implications of his *ecclesial* insistence on the removal
of racial, sexual, cultural, and economic distinctions (Rom.
13:1-7; Gal. 3:28).

This does not mean, however, that we—living in a time so different from Paul's—can neglect the catalytic power of his apocalyptic gospel and its ethical consequences. Indeed, Paul's apocalyptic faith in the transformation of the creation at the time of
God's coming reign compels an ethic that strains and labors to
move God's creation toward that future triumph of God promised in Jesus Christ and to which the presence of the Spirit
propels us.

THE CLAIM OF PAUL'S GOSPEL

The coming of the parousia, therefore, must not be evaluated in
terms of an idealistic philosophy of history, a doctrine of progress, or the possibly inherent "apocalyptic" characteristic of
human existence as an existence in hope, but in terms of the
integrity of the claim of the Pauline gospel. We simply cannot
consider ourselves to be Christians in the Pauline sense and
complacently reject his apocalyptic gospel. Inasmuch as we
claim Paul's letters to be a constituent part of our Christian con-

fession and thus to be authoritative for us as God's word, we surrender the Pauline gospel itself if we surrender its apocalyptic. And this is true because Paul's apocalyptic is part and parcel of the coherent center of Paul's gospel.

And if we argue that the pluralism and diversity of the New Testament canon leaves Christians many other options besides Paul (for instance, the Johannine option of realized eschatology), we still must face the central importance of future eschatology in the New Testament canon as a whole. In other words, even though other New Testament authors formulate the eschatological question in a way different from Paul, we cannot assert its peripheral position in the New Testament canon and so bypass its claim on us.

Moreover, it is impossible to appeal from Paul to Jesus on the ground that Jesus himself was not an apocalyptic figure. The continuous attempt by scholars to rescue Jesus from apocalyptic (for instance, Ernst Käsemann,[4] Ernst Fuchs,[5] Ethelbert Stauffer[6]) is often motivated more by a profound aversion to apocalyptic than by objective scholarship. Käsemann's observation that apocalyptic was "the mother of Christian theology"[7] cannot simply stand as a purely historical assertion. It should be translated into a theologically valid statement for the present.

The theological *claim* for Paul's apocalyptic gospel, then, is simply this: if people claim to be Pauline Christians, then they cannot surrender his apocalyptic as a disposable item because Paul's apocalyptic is part and parcel of the gospel itself. From a Pauline perspective the proclamation of Christ as our Savior and Redeemer ceases to have its authentic truth unless we adhere to its apocalyptic components.

This, to be sure, is only a "soft" claim. At this point, I do not intend to argue for a "Pauline canon within the canon of the New Testament," although the compelling power of Paul's apocalyptic gospel moves me in that direction. It could, for instance, be argued that the New Testament canon itself loses its coherent center, authenticity, and power once the centrality of

Paul's apocalyptic is suppressed. It loses its coherent center because without apocalyptic the proclamation of Christ undergoes decisive shifts. It loses its authenticity because without apocalyptic it is removed from its original eschatological mooring. And it loses its power because a gospel without apocalyptic has proved to be an abbreviated, if not distorted, gospel in the history of the church and in the church today. For it must be understood that a Christian celebrates a future apocalyptic only *because of* Christ, not *notwithstanding* Christ.

THE CONTINUING RELEVANCE OF A
FUTURE APOCALYPTIC

I have argued that a future apocalyptic is an inherent part of the Pauline gospel. A Christology that suppresses Paul's apocalyptic thrust must be characterized as a transposition to "a different gospel" (Gal. 1:6). Such a transmuted Christology is defensible only if one submits that historical change is a necessary part of the coherent core of the gospel. In that case, the core of the gospel becomes in principle a contingent structure that shifts with the demands of the times and has no permanent foundation. Christians today, then, must for the sake of the truth of the gospel and its historical continuity with the Pauline gospel *necessarily* adopt the future apocalyptic components of the gospel.

Moreover, this *necessity* is not only a commitment to the *truth-claim* of the gospel but an *existential need* as well. The future thrust of the resurrection of Christ prompts Christians to an apocalyptic self-understanding in the world. Christians live existentially in the tension of their present unfulfilled longing for that new order of God's kingdom, in which—according to Rev. 7:17—"God will wipe away every tear from their eyes." They experience that tension not only within their own bodies but also in their solidarity with all the "bodies" of our unredeemed creation. They must, therefore, yearn for the hour of the resurrection of the dead that the resurrection of Christ promises us and that will actualize God's triumph over the power of death, which poisons his creation and afflicts our bodies. Indeed, the phenomenon of hope in human life points to the need for a completion that will enable us to understand fully what we now understand only fragmentarily (1 Cor. 13:12).

In simple terms, the passion of the Christian for a redeemed creation has direct existential and ethical relevance. It deals, for instance, with the question whether such a cosmic Christian hope is more realistic and powerful than Albert Camus's conviction about "the benign indifference of the universe"[8] or Blaise Pascal's anguish when, contemplating the heavens, he cries out, "The eternal silence of these infinite spaces terrifies me."[9]

But even if we grant the necessity of, and the existential need for, an apocalyptic gospel, *has it not become untenable for us* in the face of the sheer continuation of chronological time? Indeed, the theological and existential necessity of Paul's apocalyptic gospel does run up against the frustration of chronological time. If Christians experience in their own bodies the existential and ethical tension of their present unfulfilled hope, is not that existential yearning for the triumph of God dissipated and uncovered as an illusion by the stubborn duration of time? How long can the urgency of *kairos*, the sense of a coming fulfillment of time, withstand its frustration by *chronos,* the persistent continuity of clock time? When does the promise that "the Lord is at hand" (Phil. 4:5) or "the time is near" (Rev. 1:3) become simply "not soon enough" or "sometime" or even "too late?" It makes all the difference whether the end-time is part of one's living awareness or has become part of a fixed tradition. Was the Christian church after all not correct in shifting the relation between the Christ-event and the parousia to an almost exclusive concentration on the former, or in stressing the kingdom of God as a future lure rather than as a coming certainty?

My response to this dilemma is as follows: First of all, Paul's first-century A.D. hope in the imminent coming glory of God cannot be duplicated by us in the twentieth century A.D. in the same manner. The very passage of time and our growing historical consciousness prevent us from doing so. And this is all the more true because the distance between the ground of hope, the Christ-event, and its expected actualization was as close in time for Paul as it has become distant and far-removed for us.

Second, the attempt to concentrate the focus of the gospel on chronological time has yielded not only disastrous results throughout Christian history but also an acute distortion of the core of the gospel. It has sponsored chronological speculations and predictions that not only have suffocated the primary mandates of the gospel of the incarnation but also have led to moral irresponsibility and Christian elitism.

In the third place, because we must acknowledge the difference between the stance and character of Paul's hope and ours, we cannot simply save the "imminent" character of Paul's hope by reading him, for instance, through the eyes of 2 Peter. 2 Peter attempts to come to terms with the delay of the parousia by altering the conception of time from historical chronology into a divine conception of time:

> Do not ignore this one fact, beloved, that with the Lord one day is as a thousand years, and a thousand years as one day (2 Pet. 3:8).

Such a solution ignores the urgency of time, which in Paul is motivated by the *historical* events of the death and resurrection of Christ.

In other words, the "literal" intent of Paul's apocalyptic needs to be interpreted for us on two levels. It should refer primarily to the coming actualization of God's triumph and only secondarily to its "imminent" arrival. Christians today can no longer expect with Paul the imminent arrival of the kingdom, in the same manner, because "the appointed time"—which for Paul "has grown very short" (1 Cor. 7:29)—has for us grown "very long."

This necessary readjustment of the time of the arrival of the kingdom does not call for the suspension of its coming actualization. If we were to suspend the hope in its actualization, we would destroy the very substance of Paul's gospel. And we must insist that an adjusted chronology does not signal the demise of its coming actualization.

The urgency of our hope for the end-time cannot remain authentic unless we take seriously both the cosmic-universal and temporal concerns of Paul's apocalyptic. Urgency cannot live without hope in the concrete actualization of the hoped-for object or without hope in the temporal realization of the hope. In the other words, because temporal urgency and cosmic "material" actualization are the primary elements of Paul's apocalyptic hope, its catalytic meaning for us cannot simply bypass chronological expectation altogether as if the actualization of the hope can be asserted without some form of chronological expectation as its concomitant aspect.

This becomes evident when we consider the consequences of ignoring cosmic concreteness and chronological time altogether. In that case we virtually abandon not only the concreteness and cosmic embrace of the Christian hope for the freedom of creation "from its bondage to decay" and its transformation "to the glorious liberty of the children of God" (Rom. 8:21) but also the urgent longing for its actualization, that is, the temporal dimension of the hope.

Unless Christians concentrate their hope on the *concrete occurrence* of God's final incursion into history, our hope in the coming transformation of the world is surrendered and our hope in the conquest of the structures of death in our world is made illusory. But it is also true that, unless Christians expect the coming actualization of God's promises in Christ to occur *in time,* their hope loses its passionate and realistic character. Due to the existential character of Christian hope, which cries out for deliverance from the powers of evil and death ruling our world, such hope cannot endure without some form of chronological expectation. Otherwise our stance in hope snaps and is transformed into a different mode. A hope which remains forever hope and recedes forever into the fog of the future—that is, a hope that is not related to an actualization in time—leads to sheer indifference or to an attitude of resignation—of "hanging in there." Indeed, when we simply ignore the urgency of the hope or its concrete actualization, we distort Paul's gospel and its relevance for us. In that case we usually opt for one of the following alternatives: (a) We retreat into a "private apocalypse" by translating the tension between the Christ-event and the parousia into purely existentialist terms (e.g., Bultmann). (b) We adopt some form of realized or progressive eschatology and transform the kingdom of God into a reality that either progressively actualizes itself through the church or becomes identified with the church. (c) We assume a heroic ethical stance, as if it is up to us to usher in the kingdom of God. (d) We adhere to a nonchronological promissory language (e.g., Moltmann) that, notwithstanding its emphasis on anticipation and anticipatory realization, does not address itself to either the material or the temporal aspect of the concrete incursion of the kingdom of God into our world.

CONCLUSION

Thus, notwithstanding the continuation of chronological time, Christians cannot simply take for granted its unending and enduring character. As I have stated before, chronology is only a necessary byproduct of the primary foci of Paul's apocalyptic gospel for our time. The hope for the concrete reality of God's transformation of the created order and for its actualization is grounded in the gospel of Jesus Christ, opening up the future of our world in a new way. The vision of the coming reality of God's glory compels us to a specific posture in the present, that is, to work patiently and courageously in our world in a manner dictated by the way of Christ—the way from suffering to glory. For the vision of the kingdom does not perish in the cross but is cleansed and heightened by it.

At this point let me restate my position as clearly as possible. The catalytic truth, that is, the nonliteralistic reading, of Paul's apocalyptic gospel compels us to tread the narrow path between a rigid biblicism and an exclusive existentialist interpretation of apocalyptic. A rigid biblicism wants us to resuscitate the literal apocalyptic world view of Paul with its imminent expectation. It aims at a direct transfer of biblical truth to our situation, without recognizing the gap between the biblical world and ours. Existentialism, to the contrary, overcelebrates the delay of the parousia and thus removes any "literal" dimension of Paul's apocalyptic-cosmic intent from its consideration.

Instead, we must seriously attend to the beckoning power of God's coming triumph without losing ourselves either in chronological speculations or in a denial of the coming actualization of God's promise. God's act in Christ focuses our attention on the present time as an "apocalyptic" time, that is, on the either-or of our allegiance: do we *either* serve Christ *or* the powers of this world? The apocalyptic categories of Paul's gospel focus primarily on the "now" of our decision, but *they do so only because of the motivating and beckoning power of God's final triumph.* For the "now" of our decision is only then realistic when it is inspired by the vision of God's kingdom. Without that apocalyptic vision, our hope becomes *either* a romantic illusion *or* a constrictive demand because it collapses God's coming triumph in our present personal stance and will power.

And so Paul's apocalyptic gospel opens up to us the horizon of a vision and a hope that not only contradicts our routinized understanding of life but also uncovers its cracks and thus prepares us for anchoring our life in a promise which God alone can fulfill. "For all the promises of God find their Yes in him. That is why we utter the Amen through him, to the glory of God" (2 Cor. 1:20). When we hear the statements of politicians who want to prepare us for the inevitability of a nuclear war, a psychic numbness and powerlessness threatens to engulf us. It is indeed the "apocalyptic" character of their pronouncements that frightens us because they proclaim—not unlike the neo-apocalypticists—that "they" are evil and "we" are good.

In the face of this "apocalyptic" situation, the Pauline gospel demands that we resist those apocalyptic prophets and their power because it knows the vision of another apocalyptic—the theophany of the God of Jesus Christ. That apocalypse of God calls upon us to do battle against the false apocalypses of power politics because it knows of the evil that pervades all political power. And so it calls upon us to fight for those intimations of the good that foreshadow God's ultimate triumph.

Indeed, as long as the vision of God's coming triumph inspires us, we are permitted to attend to the particularities and vicissitudes of our world. We are permitted to live the gospel in such a way that we can be radically open to the concrete demands of our fellow creatures and to the moral issues of our world. We can be sure that in and through our contingent actions and our life of compassion God will accomplish his universal design, and we may be confident that the power of death in our world will not have the last word. And so the passion for God's kingdom goes hand in hand with our compassion for our needy world.

This essay is addressed to Christians living in the world. Although it is fashionable today to stress Bultmann's shortcomings, it must be acknowledged that he, more than any other interpreter of the New Testament, understood Paul's passion for the end-time and attempted to give it existential meaning for Christians in our time. If my alternative interpretation is at all valid, it shares Bultmann's evangelical passion, albeit from a different perspective. For my interpretation does not wish to belittle the immense difficulties for Christian ministers today in proclaiming to their people God's coming cosmic triumph, transcending the need for a purely personal integrity in the midst of a world that mocks any cosmic implications of the Christian hope. When I nevertheless posit this alternative, it is in the conviction that the cosmic implications of Paul's gospel drive us out of our cultural ghettos—to the larger concerns of our interdependent and pluralistic world. Moreover, I am convinced that the oppressive structures of the powers of sin and death in our world cry out for that world of righteousness and glory that God has promised us in Christ.

And so the delay of the parousia both motivates us and aggravates us; it inspires both a great impatience and a patient endurance. It *motivates* us to discern God's radical transcendence over all our wishes and expectations. It also motivates us to continue to work patiently in preparation for that coming reign of God that according to his purpose and promise in Christ will be our glorious destiny.

But it also *aggravates* us because of the onslaught of the power of sin and death in our world, because of the groaning and suffering of the creation within us and around us. And so we must continue to be agitators for the kingdom, joyful that in Christ we may detect and erect some signs of its dawning, and yet burdened because God's triumph has not yet defeated the awful powers of injustice, suffering, and death in our world.

Our common Christian life in the world involves an inescapable tension—a tension gravitating between joy and agony. We rejoice in the "already" that is, in the presence of the love of God that in Christ embraces our lives and enables us to anticipate his coming glory; but we also agonize because of the terrifying "not yet," that is, the uncompleted character of God's presence that grips the lives of so many of God's creatures, overwhelming them and often destroying them. And although others may come to terms with "the permanent human condition," Christians are not permitted to do so. Their lives must be a constant prayer of "Our Lord, come" (1 Cor. 16:22) in response to the promise of Paul's gospel:

> God is faithful, by whom you were called into the fellowship of his son, Jesus Christ (1 Cor. 1:9).

And I am sure that he who began a good work in you will bring it to completion at the day of Jesus Christ (Phil. 1:6).

And so Christians in their own way join the liturgy of the synagogue: "I believe with complete conviction in the appearance of the messiah, and even if he tarries I will nevertheless daily await his coming."[10]

Notes

CHAPTER 1

1. Albert Schweitzer, *The Quest of the Historical Jesus: A Critical Study of Its Progress from Reimarus to Wrede,* Eng. trans. W. Montgomery, 3d ed. (New York: Macmillan, 1961), pp. 370–71.
2. *United Presbyterian A.D.* (October 1981): 16.
3. *United Presbyterian A.D.* (December 1981): 8.

CHAPTER 2

1. Robert Jewett, *Jesus Against the Rapture: Seven Unexpected Prophecies* (Philadelphia: Westminster Press, 1979), p. 138.
2. Gilbert Murray, *Five Stages of Greek Religion* (Garden City, N.Y.: Doubleday & Co., 1955), chap. 4.
3. See Hans Schwarz, *On the Way to the Future: A Christian View of Eschatology in the Light of Current Trends in Religion,* rev. ed. (Minneapolis: Augsburg, 1979), p. 156.
4. Hal Lindsey, *The Late Great Planet Earth* (Grand Rapids: Zondervan, 1970), p. 6.
5. Ibid., p. 18.
6. Ibid., p. 41.
7. Ibid., pp. 157ff.
8. Jewett, *Jesus Against the Rapture,* p. 23.
9. Daniel L. Migliore, "Theology of Hope," unpublished lecture, Princeton Theological Seminary (Fall 1979).
10. Ibid.
11. Ibid.

CHAPTER 3

1. Ernst Käsemann, " 'The Righteousness of God' in Paul," *New Testament Questions of Today,* Eng. trans. W.J. Montague (Philadelphia: Fortress Press, 1969), pp. 168-82.

2. Dieter Lührmann, *Glaube im frühen Christentum* (Gütersloh: G. Mohn, 1976).

3. Ernst Käsemann, *Perspectives on Paul,* Eng. trans. Margaret Kohl (Philadelphia: Fortress Press, 1971), p. 27.

4. William Wrede, *Paul,* Eng. trans. Edward Lummis (London: Philip Green, 1907), pp. 105-6, 111.

5. Rudolf Bultmann, *Primitive Christianity in Its Contemporary Setting,* Eng. trans. R.H. Fuller (Philadelphia: Fortress Press, 1980), p. 186.

6. John Macquarrie, *Christian Hope* (New York: Seabury Press, 1978), p. 32.

CHAPTER 5

1. James M. Robinson, "The Future of New Testament Theology," *Religious Studies Review* 2 (January 1976): 17-23.

2. Ernst Käsemann, "On the Subject of Primitive Christian Apocalyptic," *New Testament Questions of Today,* Eng. trans. W.J. Montague (Philadelphia: Fortress Press, 1969), p. 137.

3. Joseph A. Fitzmyer, *Pauline Theology: A Brief Sketch* (Englewood Cliffs, N.J.: Prentice-Hall, 1967).

4. E.P. Sanders, *Paul and Palestinian Judaism: A Comparison of Patterns of Religion* (Philadelphia: Fortress Press, 1977), p. 523.

5. Robinson, "The Future of New Testament Theology," p. 18.

6. C.H. Dodd, *The Meaning of Paul for Today* (Cleveland: World Publishing Co., 1957) and *The Apostolic Preaching and Its Developments,* 2d ed. (New York: Harper & Row, 1951); J.A.T. Robinson, *Jesus and His Coming: The Emergence of a Doctrine,* 2d ed. (Philadelphia: Westminster Press, 1979) and *The Body: A Study in Pauline Theology,* Studies in Biblical Theology 5 (London: SCM Press, 1952).

7. Gerd Lüdemann, *Paulus, der Heidenapostel,* Band I, *Studien zur Chronologie* (Göttingen: Vandenhoeck & Ruprecht, 1980).

8. Rudolf Bultmann, "New Testament and Mythology," *Kerygma and Myth: A Theological Debate,* ed. H.W. Bartsch and Eng. trans. R.H. Fuller (New York: Harper & Row, Torchbooks, 1961), p. 41.

9. Ibid., p. 36.

10. Cf. Rudolf Bultmann, *Theology of the New Testament,* vol. I, Eng. trans. Kendrick Grobel (New York: Charles Scribner's Sons, 1951), p. viii.

11. Oscar Cullmann, *Christ and Time: The Primitive Christian Conception of Time and History,* Eng. trans. Floyd V. Filson, rev. ed. (Philadelphia: Westminster Press, 1964), *The Christology of the New Testament,* Eng. trans. S.C. Guthrie and C.A.M. Hall (Philadelphia: Westminster Press, 1959), and *Salvation in History,* Eng. trans. Sidney G. Sowers et al. (New York: Harper & Row, 1967).

12. Cullmann, *Christ and Time,* p. 84.

13. Ibid., p. 139.

CHAPTER 6

1. Rudolph Bultmann, "New Testament and Mythology," *Kerygma and Myth: A Theological Debate,* ed. H.W. Bartsch and Eng. trans. R.H. Fuller (New York: Harper & Row, Torchbooks, 1961), pp. 1–44.

2. Paul Ricoeur, *Essays on Biblical Interpretation,* edited with an Introduction by Lewis S. Mudge (Philadelphia: Fortress Press, 1980), p. 8.

3. Rudolf Bultmann, *Primitive Christianity in Its Contemporary Setting,* Eng. trans. R.H. Fuller (Philadelphia: Fortress Press, 1980), p. 186 and 208.

4. C.H. Dodd, *The Meaning of Paul for Today* (Cleveland: World Publishing Co., 1957); Walter Rauschenbusch, *A Theology for the Social Gospel* (Nashville: Abingdon Press, 1979).

5. Mircea Eliade, *The Myth of the Eternal Return,* Eng. trans. Willard R. Trask (Princeton: Princeton University Press, 1971), pp. 106, 111, 112.

6. Vittorio Lanternari, *The Religions of the Oppressed: A Study of Modern Messianic Cults,* Eng. trans. Lisa Sergio (New York: Alfred A. Knopf, 1963).

7. Peter Worsley, *The Trumpet Shall Sound* (London: MacGibbon and Kee, 1957).

8. John Gager, *Kingdom and Community: The Social World of Early Christianity* (Englewood Cliffs, N.J.: Prentice-Hall, 1975), p. 39.

9. Leon Festinger et al., *When Prophecy Fails* (Minneapolis: University of Minnesota Press, 1956), p. 28.

10. Yonina Talmon, "Pursuit of the Millennium: The Relationship between Religious and Social Change," *Reader in Comparative*

Religion: An Anthropological Approach, eds. W. Lessa and E. Vogt, 2d ed. (New York: Harper & Row, 1965), p. 522.

11. Jonathan Z. Smith, "A Pearl of Great Price and a Cargo of Yams: A Study in Situational Incongruity," *History of Religions* 16 (1976): 1–19.

12. Talman, p. 529; see also, Bryan R. Wilson, *Sects and Society* (Berkeley, Ca.: University of California Press, 1961).

13. Martin Werner, *The Formation of Christian Dogma: An Historical Study of the Problem,* Eng. trans. S.G.F. Brandon (New York: Harper & Row, 1957).

14. John Macquarrie, "Eschatology and Time," *The Future of Hope,* ed. Frederick Herzog (New York: Herder and Herder, 1970), pp. 115–16; italics mine.

15. C.H. Dodd, *The Apostolic Preaching and Its Developments,* 2d ed. (New York: Harper & Row, 1951), pp. 65–66.

16. Rudolf Bultmann, *Jesus Christ and Mythology* (New York: Charles Scribner's Sons, 1958); and Bultmann, "New Testament and Mythology."

17. Amos N. Wilder, *Eschatology and Ethics in the Teachings of Jesus* (New York: Harper & Row, 1950), p. 160.

18. Norman Perrin, *Jesus and the Language of the Kingdom* (Philadelphia: Fortress Press, 1976), pp. 43–56.

19. Cf. Schubert M. Ogden, *Christ without Myth* (New York: Harper & Row, 1961).

20. Cf. Daniel D. Williams, *God's Grace and Man's Hope* (New York: Harper & Row, 1949).

21. William A. Beardslee, "Hope in Biblical Eschatology and in Process Theology," *Journal of the American Academy of Religion* 38 (September 1970): 227–39. See also, "Openness to the New in Apocalyptic and in Process Theology," *Process Studies* 3 (1973): 169–78.

22. Macquarrie, "Eschatology and Time," p. 124.

23. Robert Jewett, *Jesus Against the Rapture: Seven Unexpected Prophecies* (Philadelphia: Westminster Press, 1979), pp. 29–30, 63.

24. Richard H. Hiers, *Jesus and the Future: Unsolved Questions on Eschatology* (Atlanta: John Knox Press, 1981), p. 108.

25. Dieter Zeller, "Exegese als Anstosz für die systematische Eschatologie: Zusammenfassende Überlegungen," *Gegenwart und Kommendes Reich,* Schulergabe Anton Vögtle, ed. Peter Fiedler and Dieter Zeller (Stuttgart: Verlag Katholisches Bibelwerk, 1975), p. 157.

26. Wolfhart Pannenberg, *Jesus—God and Man,* Eng. trans. L.L. Wilkins and D.A. Priebe (Philadelphia: Westminster Press, 1968), pp. 232–34, 249–50.

27. Cf. Jürgen Moltmann, *Theology of Hope,* Eng. trans. James W. Leitch (New York: Harper & Row, 1967).

28. Karl Barth, *The Epistle to the Romans,* Eng. trans. Edwyn C. Hoskyns (London: Oxford University Press, 1933).

29. Karl Barth, *Church Dogmatics* II/1, ed. G.W. Bromiley and T.F. Torrance (Edinburgh: T. & T. Clark, 1957), pp. 621–40.

30. Macquarrie, "Eschatology and Time," pp. 115–16.

CHAPTER 7

1. G.W.H. Lampe, "Early Patristic Eschatology," *Eschatology: Four Papers Read to the Society for the Study of Theology* (Edinburgh: Oliver and Boyd, 1952), p. 19.

2. Ibid., p. 21.

3. See Jaroslav Pelikan, *The Christian Tradition: A History of the Development of Doctrine,* vol. 1: *The Emergence of the Catholic Tradition* (Chicago: University of Chicago Press, 1971), p. 55.

4. Ernst Käsemann, "The Beginnings of Christian Theology," *New Testament Questions of Today,* Eng. trans. W.J. Montague (Philadelphia: Fortress Press, 1969), p. 101.

5. Ernst Fuchs, "The Quest of the Historical Jesus," *Studies of the Historical Jesus,* Eng. trans. Andrew Scobie, Studies in Biblical Theology 42 (London: SCM Press, 1964), pp. 11–31.

6. Ethelbert Stauffer, *Jesus and His Story.* Eng. trans. Richard and Clara Winston (New York: Alfred A. Knopf, 1960), pp. 160ff.

7. Käsemann, "The Beginnings of Christian Theology," p. 102.

8. Albert Camus, *The Stranger,* Eng. trans. Stuart Gilbert (New York: Alfred A. Knopf, 1946), p. 154.

9. Blaise Pascal, *Pensées,* Eng. trans. W.F. Trotter (New York: E.P. Dutton, 1958), p. 61.

10. Pinchas Lapide and Jürgen Moltmann, *Jewish Monotheism and Christian Trinitarian Doctrine: A Dialogue,* Eng. trans. Leonard Swindler (Philadelphia: Fortress Press, 1981), p. 86.